Sacred Roots

Commonalities expressed

by the Early

Church and Synagogue

by

Dr.Albert Plotkin, D.H.L.,D.D., LL.D

Fogfree, Inc. Publisher

Text by
Dr. Albert Plotkin

This book is dedicated to the loving memory of my dear wife, Sylvia, our daughter Debra Ruth and in honor of my devoted daughter, Janis Lee

Foreword by
Bishop Thomas O'Brien

Edited by Karl Pohlhaus & Jina Asulin

Illustrated by
Temple Beth Israel
Our thanks to Temple Beth Israel for supplying the pictures for the front and back covers

ISBN NUMBER: 0-9713823-3-6

Author Rabbi Plotkin

Foreword

Most Rev. Thomas J. O'Brien, Bishop of Phoenix

   As a priest and bishop for over forty years, my life has been enriched through my interaction with many faith filled men and women from both Christian and Non-Christian religious traditions. I have experienced the blessings of friendship, dialogue and new insights as I have gotten to know many of the other religious leaders who have dedicated their lives in ministry to the people of Arizona. One of those people who has graced my life by sharing his faith with me, Rabbi Albert Plotkin, has also been one of the most significant.

II

One of my strongest commitments, as bishop, has been to consistently promote both ecumenical and inter religious relationships. While there can be legitimate differences in how different faith traditions understand and express the profound encounters with God that are announced in the scriptures, all benefit when our reflective insights on the nature of God, who exceeds all human understanding and expression, are shared in ways that are mutually respectful In the "*Declaration on the Relation of the Church to Non-Christian Religions, Nostra Aetate*," taken from the Second Vatican Council, the Catholic Church has stated, "Dialogue presupposed that each side wishes to know the other, and wishes to increase and deepen its knowledge of the other. It constitutes a particularly suitable means of favoring a better mutual knowledge and, especially in the case of dialogue between Jews and Christians, of probing the riches of one's own tradition. Dialogue demands respect for the other as he is; above all, respect for his faith and his religious convictions."

In the Hebrew scriptures, Jews and Christians share a common sacred tradition. The story of the Jewish people, of God's intervention in history and the expressions found there of God's will to reveal himself as a God who saves, is our story too. Much can be gained through joint study of the biblical texts by combined groups of Jewish and Christian scholars.

Rabbi Plotkin brings a different perspective to our efforts at mutual understanding by examining the worship practices of our two traditions. Perhaps his efforts can be a stimulus for a reflective Christian response that promotes further dialogue, leading to a deeper level of understanding and appreciation on the part of both Jews and Christians. I am grateful for his efforts in providing this resource.

Most Reverend Thomas J. O'Brien
Bishop of Phoenix, Arizona

Table of Contents

About the Author

Albert Plotkin was born and raised in South Bend, Indiana. When it came time to attend college he chose Notre Dame University close by, graduating from that school with a Magna Cum Luada and B.A. Degree in 1942. Later he would note that he was the only Jewish Rabbi to go to this citadel of Roman Catholic learning. After college he attended the Hebrew Union Seminary, graduating with a Master of Hebrew letters in 1948. In 1967 the Hebrew Union Seminary awarded him a Doctor of Hebrew Letters. In 1973 he received a Doctor of Divinity degree. His first pastoral assignment was as an assistant Rabbi in Seattle, Washington in 1948. During his Rabbinate he met and married his wife.

In 1949 he was called to Spokane, Washington to take the position of chief Rabbi of Temple Emmanuel. During this term Albert became extremely ecumenical and socially involved in the greater Spokane area. In 1955 Temple Beth Israel called him to serve as Rabbi in Phoenix, Arizona. This pastorate lasted for 38 years from 1955 to 1991. Along the way, Arizona State University awarded him a Doctorate of Law degree to show their appreciation for his contribution to the greater community. Upon retiring from Temple Beth Israel, a Jewish community called him to start a new Temple in Sedona, Arizona. From 1991 to the present he has served the Sedona community. Soon a Temple will appear in Sedona, the fruits of his faithful service. This book was started in 1947 and completed 40 years later.

CHAPTER ONE
Jewish Origins In Early Church practices

1) Jewish origins of the Golden Rule

Jesus lived in a Jewish environment. He was himself a student of the Torah and the Prophets. A son of the Synagogue, he often went to teach, preach, and learn there. It is reasonable to assume that many of the teachings, which later were written in the Mishnah, Talmud or Midrash existed in his time, because there are no grounds whatsoever for assuming that the Gospels influenced the authorities of the Talmud and Midrash. There are ethical sayings that attribute to Jesus, recurring word for word, in the Talmud and Midrash. For example, the saying, *"With what measure will you mete it out, shall it be meted out to you,"* is in the Sermon on the Mount and we find it exactly word for word in the Talmud. There are other sayings, that have parallels in the Talmud, as well as the Tanakh, as well as other books of Jewish tradition.

In Matthew 7:7-11 we have this most beautiful teaching: *"Ask, and it shall be given you; seek, and ye shall find, Knock, and it shall be opened unto you: For everyone that asketh receiveth; and he that seeketh findeth; and to him that knocketh it shall be opened. Or what man is there of you, whom if his son ask bread, will he give him a stone? Or if he asks a fish, will he give him a serpent? Of course no one would! So if you, shiftless as you are, know how to give good gifts unto your children, how much more shall your Father, who is in heaven, give good things to the man that asks him?"* Further in this quotation, we have an understanding of how every child knows by instinct what his parents will give him. Likewise, men know by instinct that the gifts of God are for their benefit. The Rabbis teach the same lesson: *"Whatever God does, is entirely good"*

(Berachoth, 60B) *"God never deals harshly with his creatures"* (AvodaZara 3A) That God is as merciful as man, is repeatedly emphasized by scripture: *"Like as a father pities his children, so the Lord pities those that fear him."* (Psalm 103:13). Another parallel is given by Ecclesiates, which contrasts human sympathy, which is limited, with divine mercy, which is infinite. *"The mercy of man is upon his neighbor, but mercy of the Lord is upon all flesh."* The Jew who wrote Estras entreats divine pity for the many, of whom only a few will be chosen. He is assured that God's mercy and love exceeds that of man. *"For you who come far short, should you be able to love my creatures more than I ?"* This is earlier than the Gospels but most likely Jesus must have heard it in his time, for he included it as part of his basis teachings.

Philo, the great Jewish Philosopher of Alexandria speaks of God being towards the world what parents are to their children. In his study on special laws, he refers again and again to the analogy that exists between our parents on earth and our Father in heaven. The injunction to pray is mentioned three times "Ask - seek - knock" in order to emphasize the duty of prayer. He has promised his disciples that their prayers shall be answered by God. *"Ask and it shall be given"*- there is no qualification. This was a deep belief of the Jews at that time; namely, that prayer has great power, is given to all, and that all one needs to do is to participate and the prayers will be answered.

The phrase *"Seek and ye shall find"* has probably been borrowed from Proverbs 8:17 *"and those who seek me early shall find me."* Or the Prophet Jeremiah 29:13 *"And ye shall seek me, and find me"* Isaiah also has a similar passage (65:6). *"Seek the Lord while he may be found".* Thus, all through the Bible we find continual references to the fact that God can be found if you seek Him. It is all there and ready for every human being to seek and achieve. The most famous of all quotations of the Sermon on the Mount is the following: *"Therefore all things, whatsoever you would that men should do to you, do you even so to them for this is the law and the Prophets."* (Matthew 7:12)

Luke's parallel is slightly different: *"And as you would, that men should do to you, do you also to them likewise."* (Luke 6:31) Here the emphasis is on a mutual love and respect for all human life and this became the basis of the Golden Rule. The Golden Rule is actually a reinterpretation or paraphrase from the Torah found in Leviticus 19:18 *"Love your neighbor as yourself."* In the book of Tobit, Chapter 4 verse 15 *"And what you yourself hate, do to no man"*. This is identical with the expression of Hillel, who lived a hundred years before Jesus, when he said in the Talmud (Sabbath 31A): *"What is hateful unto yourself do not to your neighbor"*. Here is a negative rule which is still preserved in Rabbinic literature and also in the Aramaic Book of the Talmud, the Arramay book of the Bible, and the Targun in which Onkelos makes this statement: *"A man should show love to his fellow man by not doing to him what he dislikes when done to himself."*

Thus, the Talmud gives us the very foundation stone of the Golden Rule, and in the Sermon on the Mount, we note that Matthew emphasizes that it comes from the Torah and the Prophets. These were the books, which Jesus studied and knew well. He refers to them constantly as they are the very foundation of his love and his teaching.

The origin of Hillel's and Jesus' version of the Golden Rule is the positive commandment of Leviticus 19:18 *"To love your neighbor as yourself"*. It is a source of several forms of the Golden Rule found in Jewish literature. Rabbi A. Elazar Ben Arach says: *"Let your neighbor's honor be as dear to you as your own"*(Avot 2:15)

In Avot DE Rabbi Nathan expanded this saying in the following manner: *"Just as a man sees to his own honor and reputation, so let him see to his neighbor's, and just as he does not like an evil report to be spread about concerning his own character, so let him desire not to spread an evil report concerning his neighbor's."* This is interesting because we have the positive and the negative form combined. Another rabbi paraphrased the Mosaic Law of life in this verse: *"Let the property of your neighbor be as dear to you as your own".* (Avot 2:17) This is also positive. *"Again, just as a man looks with a good eye upon his own home, so let him look upon the home of his neighbor in the same way."* (Avot DE Rabbi Nathan 16:62)

In addition to these positive forms of the Golden Rule, there is another one in the Book of Ecclesiates 31:15 *"Consider your neighbor's likings as your own".*

Analogies to the Golden Rule can be found in other religions but with this difference. While like the teachings of Jesus, the rule assumes a positive form, in all other known instances, it is given negatively. The negative confines us to the region of justice: the positive takes us into the realm of generosity; for we wish more than we can claim the average man is willing to do for others.

Judaism is a simple system of ethics and not a book of philosophy or theology. Hillel had to meet the test of a heathen, who needed a summary of Jewish teachings best calculated to bring home to him the unworthy attitude he had adopted. What could be more practical than the negative form of the Golden Rule: *"What was hateful to you to suffer at the hands of another, do not do to your fellow man".* (Sabbath 31A). Eusebius has preserved a similar form of the rule used by Philo: *"Moreover, it is ordained in the Torah that no one shall do to his neighbor what he would be unwilling to have done to himself."* Even though the teaching on love in Leviticus 19:18 is paraphrased in the

Golden Rule, the fact that it occurs eight times in the Gospels, testifies to its imperishable value as the fundamental law of life and religion.

We can understand why Rabbi Akiba considered this precept, *"Love your neighbor as yourself"* as the all-inclusive summary of the law. His contemporary, Simeon Ben Azzai agreed that this law of love was the summary of all the Torah and that it is the fulfillment of the verse from Genesis 5:1 *"This is the book of humanity"*. Thus, we know that this Golden Rule was the basic foundation stone both for Jesus and the rabbis. It became the keynote of the heart of the Law and its regard for all human beings. This foundation stone of the teaching of Jesus can best be understood when we see it in relationship to the rabbis and the Talmud.

2) **Jewish origins of the Lord's Prayer**

The Lord's Prayer in the Gospels can be derived from many of the early prayers of the Jewish Community. The very concept of prayer in the New Testament followed very much in the creative spirit of the Jewish Community. It is well to understand that each line of the Lord's Prayer has its roots in Judaism, as a shortened version of a number of Jewish prayers, put together into simple form. It is today the most important prayer in both the Catholic and Protestant rituals.

The Lord's Prayer is distinctly Jewish in structure. As regards to its content, the same conclusion can be drawn when we are able to demonstrate how all of the phrases and petitions have been borrowed from Jewish sources.

The first verse begins with *"Our Father who art in Heaven, hallowed be thy name" "Our Father in Heaven"* is Jewish in spirit and content. It uses the words, which are common in every Jewish prayer of the Abinu Shebbashamayim. This was the way God was addressed during Jesus' time. We find many examples in the Psalms and other prayers, recited prior to Jesus' birth, that reference God as Father. We begin with the prayer in eighteen common benedictions: *"God of our Fathers, God of Abraham, Isaac and Jacob."* This is a common form of expression that we also find in Exodus 4:22 where God is addressed as Father. The Jewish Liturgy uses the term often. It is frequently spoken today and in the High Holy Liturgy we address God as our *"Father and our King."* The concept of God as Father was used not only in Rabbinic literature, but also in the Books of Deuteronomy, Isaiah, Jeremiah, and Malachi. We are able to conclude that the concept of Father is a common link between both the Jewish and Christian Liturgy. God is addressed in both traditions in the same manner.

The next phrase is *"Hallowed be thy name"*. The best parallel to this is the opening phrase of the Kaddish in the words *"Magnified and hallowed be His name."* The Kaddish is often referred to in Rabbinic writings as words of praise in honor of God's Kingdom. We know that the opening phrase of the Kaddish is based on Ezekiel 28:23 *"I will magnify myself and sanctify myself, I will make known in the eyes of many nations; and they shall know that I am the Lord."* Another parallel to hallowed be thy name is found in Psalms 111 verse 9 *"Holy and revered is His name."* The ideal of Jewish life is summoned up in the expression "Kaddish Hashim." Sanctifying God's name implies absolute love and loyalty to God and to his will. In Chapter 29:23 Isaiah foretells the return of Jacob to the fold through faith; and then *"they shall sanctify my name; yea, they shall sanctify the holy one of Jacob".* The third benediction of the eighteen prayers, the Shemoneh Esreh is based on Isaiah 6:3. We may appreciate that what Jesus used in his prayer, was and still is a common link between Jewish and Christian prayers of sanctification.

6

The next verse *"Thy kingdom come,"* again follows the Kaddish *"may He establish His kingdom soon.."* In the eleventh benediction of the Shemoneh Esreh, we find a further parallel: *"and reign over us, thou alone."* It is often being pointed out, according to Rabbinic teaching *"every benediction to be valid, must contain not only the name of God but also refer to God's kingdom.."* (The Talmud Berachot, 40B) The general form of a benediction is *"Blessed art Thou oh Lord our God, King of the universe".* This clearly implies the universal rule of God based on the greatest of all facts: that He alone is Lord and also holds that He is God, Creator and Father in whose image we have been made and created. God's Kingdom on earth has not been realized. The greatest obstacle is man's sin and pride, exhibited in preferring his own will to the will of God. The kingdom of pride will be completely overthrown when the Messianic Age is fulfilled.

The next petition is *"Thy will be done on earth as it is in Heaven".* What better parallel do we have then in Psalm 135:6 where it states, *"Whatsoever pleased the Lord, that did he in heaven, and on earth".* In Rabbinic literature we find many parallels. As Rabbi Gamaliel use to say *"Do God's will as if it were your will, that He may do your will as it is written His will."* Judah Bentema said, *"Be strong as a leopard, light as an eagle, fleet as a heart and strong as a lion to the will of your Father who is in heaven.."* The Talmud says *"The man who has bread in his basket for today and then asks: 'what shall I do for tomorrow's bread?,' belongs to the people of little faith.."* *"God makes the days and provides it sustenance,"* say the words from the Mechilta.

"Give us this day our daily bread" also can be understood from the experience recorded in the Book of Exodus on the giving of manna. *"Behold I will rain bread from heaven for you, and the people shall go out and gather*

a day's portion each day." The last words were interpreted by the rabbi as follows, Rabbi Joshua said: *"A day's portion everyday meant that a man should gather on one day for the next as on Friday for Saturday."* Rabbi Eliezer Hamodai said: *"it meant that a man should not gather on one day for the next day, because it is said the portion for each day rests on it's day."* Another parallel to the Matthew version to the prayer is taken from the prophet Isaiah 33:16 *"His bread shall be given him; his water shall be sure."* Naturally, in the grace after meals, Jews thank God for the food, which he feeds and sustains us continually day by day. Thus, we note that this prayer is very much a prayer that Jews recite after the meal in giving thanks to God for our daily bread.

The next verse *"forgive us our debts as we forgive our debtors"* has a common basis in Jewish benedictions. This is practically the same word that is pronounced in the sixth benediction of the Shemoneh Esreh, *"Forgive us, our Father, for we have sinned, pardon our transgressions."* The rabbis constantly taught that it is necessary for every human being to meet his obligations, as between one human being and another, as it is to discharge his debt to God. Rabbi Ben Sirach recited the words *"Forgive your neighbor the hurt which he has done unto you, so shall your sins be pardoned when you pray."* Also in the Talmud, it states *"God says, that though the transgressor of thy sins is forgiven by me, go thee to the creditor and ask his pardon as well."* The lesson of forgiveness is found in the Book of the Testaments of the Twelve Patriarchs; *"Love each one as brother and put hatred away from your heart; love one another in deed, and in word, and in the inclination of your soul. Love you therefore one another from the heart and if a man sins against you, cast forth the poison of hate and speak peacefully to him and in thy soul hold no guile; and if he confesses, repent and forgive him."*

We see that the concept of deliverance from evil is

primarily the hope of both Judaism and Christianity. It is interesting to study the problem of temptation from the Jewish as well as the Christian perspective. In the Lord's Prayer, it seems that the devil is the author of man's temptations; but in the Jewish prayer the evil inclination within a man's heart is the source of all evil. The Jewish view is based on Genesis 8:21 which says; *"For the imagination of man's heart is evil from his youth,"* which teaches that evil comes from the imaginations of the heart. Throughout the whole of Jewish theology, the devil plays a comparative small role, compared with that assigned to him in Christian theology. Already in the Talmud, Satan is identified as the *Yezer Hara*, the evil inclination within us. This evil inclination must not be conceived as having an independent existence outside of man's heart, nor is it a prayer at war with God. It is often to be understood as one who turns from God to an evil inclination.

We note that the prayer ends in a doxology, *"Thine is the kingdom, and the power, and the glory forever."* The original source of this doxology was taken from First Chronicles 29:11, *"Thine, O Lord, is the greatness, and the power, and the glory, for Thine is the kingdom."* doxologies are by no means uncommon in Jewish literature. In the Psalms we find that at the end of each of the four books a benediction is said. The last books conclude with a Psalm that is a doxology. In the Temple, the people did not use the word *"Amen"* as a response, but said, *"Blessed be His name whose glorious kingdom is forever and ever."* Thus, we are able to demonstrate the many parallels between the Lord's Prayer and Jewish Prayers. In many instances there is no question that the Lord's Prayer was and still is a Jewish prayer. It likely may have been a combination of many different Jewish prayers put together so that the prayer could be taught in a simple fashion. This brief demonstration provides an understanding of the spiritual link between the two faiths. Understanding the Jewish sources may be the best way to understand the true and profound meaning of the Lord's Prayer we seek to teach.

3) The Jewish Origin of the Eucharistic Prayer

To understand the Jewish origin of the Eucharist, we need to go to the earliest form of church service. We find it in the Didache, one of the most impressive texts of Christian antiquity. This little manual was simultaneously a work of catechism, liturgy, and discipline for the early Church. The text of this work, which occupies an intermediate position between the New Testament and the Apostolic Fathers, was discovered in 1873 by Philotheos Bryennios, the Greek Metropolitan of Nicomedia in the library of the Monastery of the Holy Sepulcher in Constantinople. The Metropolitan dignitary has a most interesting discussion of the structure of how the early Church observed the Eucharist service.

In studying the background of the early Church service, we note that already in the 4th Century, the Church had established a set system, whereby they gathered first in a celebration with thanksgiving over a cup of wine, followed by another thanksgiving over the bread. At the end of the liturgy there was another longer thanksgiving prayer which is very similar to the Birkat Ha-Mazon, the prayer that concludes the Jewish ritual meal, and is considered to be a text from which the Eucharist prayer itself derives. It is, in fact, a prayer of thanksgiving, from the Sabbath service, particularly as it pertains to the blessing over the wine and bread, and concluded, as one does in a traditional service, by giving thanks through the Birkat Ha-Mazon. That was recited by the people who were at the meal. In time this was taken over by the early Church, likely because many of the initial members were Jews who were used to this kind of prayer service. The interesting part of the Eucharistic service is that it follows very much in the tradition of Judaism. Admittedly, the contemporary Church has become conscious of the fact that it needs to go back into its early beginnings to understand the roots from which these important elements of the faith sprang up.

A particularly interesting part of the service spoken of in the Didache is the Prayer of Thanksgiving. The prayer begins with the words: *"When your hunger has been satisfied, give thanks unto God and be grateful for His blessing."* The use of the prayer of the early Church indicated that they wanted to give thanks to God after they finished the meal. That was done as a community and so used the same language as the older prayer, but with a Christianized ending, giving thanks to God through Christ Jesus. From this, one may appreciate that the origin of the prayer of Thanksgiving spoken after the meal, and found in the Didache, shows the influence of a former tradition.

It was the work of the late Dr. Louis Finkelstein who, while studying the Didache, found in it the very heart of the Birkat Ha-Mazon. The Birkat Ha-Mazon is divided into three paragraphs:

(1)first a blessing of God who feeds us,
(2)secondly, an act of thanksgiving for the gifts of Land and food
(3)thirdly, a petitionary prayer for Jerusalem.

The late Dr. Louis Finkelstein compared the text of the Birkat Ha-Mazon with the Didache to conclude that the two texts are parallel. He sees this parallel as a proof that at the time of the Jewish prayer the Birkat Ha-Mazon had only three blessings. For Finkelstein, the Didache in chapter 10, even though it is a Christian text, testifies to the Jewish tradition of the Birkat Ha-Mazon. Finkelstein shows how the Birkat Ha-Mazon was a prayer of Thanksgiving, which the community felt compelled to recite after they had finished the meal and had completed the service.

Among studies on the Didache, Finkelstein's textual conclusions show that there is a transition from Judaism to Christianity in the Birkat Ha-Mazon as it went through a number of changes that put into it a more Christian setting for the early Church.

It is my view, as I have studied the Didache, that it fits in with its Jewish origin. First, by giving the blessing of thanksgiving over the wine, then by giving the blessing over the bread, and then, at the conclusion of the meal. There were a number of other prayers that are part of the traditional Birkat Ha-Mazon located in this prayer book. The Didache affirms that the news brought by Jesus consisted in the revelation of a new place of worship and a new liturgy. The Temple is no longer a building, but the heart of the faithful. The new liturgy consists in the act of calling upon God. God the Father, through Jesus, reveals the deepest nature of Israel and the Temple, creating an act of salvation that brings as its fruits: knowledge, faith, life and immortality.

The Birkat Ha-Mazon comes at the end of the Jewish ritual meal. It begins with praise and blessing for the nourishment, acknowledging that God gives to all. It is the religious experience of that meal that suggests this theme with which the Didache prayer speaks in almost identical words. Those who have partaken of the meal are ever grateful to God and give thanks to him with their whole heart, for now they have found a new bond in their relationship with God, the relationship of eternal life, a life that consists of partaking of the spiritual food and drink and giving thanks together as a community. This then became part of the new Christian service.

We now know that the text of the Didache had its parallel source in the Birkat Ha-Mazon. There is also a passage from the book of Jubilees, a text of Essene origin, put together for the most part in the century before Jesus. It states, *"And he ate and drank and blessed the most high God who had created Heaven and earth and all the abundance of the earth and had given it to the children of men that they might eat, drink and bless their Creator."*

This attitude is central to the Birkat Ha-Mazon and, of course, is attested to by the book of Jubilees, an apocryphal book, found in the Dur Europus monument in Iraq. In the early Church, Paul says that the rite of the Jewish meal God created, is to be received with thanksgiving by the believers who know the Truth. We can see in these rites a specific intention for God. In the rite of the Jewish meal, one must eat with thanksgiving. That is the central point of the Birkat Ha-Mazon. Here, we see how the Jewish people are always mindful of the fact that when they have finished, they need to give thanks. That too, became a central part of the ritual of the early Church. It attests to a quote from the Torah. In the book of Deuteronomy, Chapter 8:10 it reads: *"When you have eaten your fill, then you must bless your God."* This quotation from Deuteronomy is based on the obligation of reciting the Birkat Ha-Mazon and demonstrates the value of this rite, later to be adopted by the early Church as an important part of the Eucharistic ritual.

The early Church, following its Jewish roots, first gathered together to thank God as Jesus had said to them, *"do this in memory of Me"*. How these words are interpreted provides a point of departure from the historic Christian understanding. These are words that are held sacred by many millions of Christians around the world. But the historic evidence, from the Jewish perspective, of one Jewish leader/rabbi telling his followers to celebrate a Jewish ritual meal exclusively in memory of him, presents contradictions to the Jewish mind. Those who are Jews by origin, have practiced this tradition in their homes for

13

many centuries. No one needs to establish a memory for a rite that has been practiced for centuries. The Jewish understanding of this text is simply that Jesus wished his followers to continue to observe this rite remembering what he had taught them until they could all celebrate their salvation in God's eternal kingdom. The change in emphasis likely came into the text at some time in the second century when it was not considered fashionable to refer to Jewish traditions.

We note that in the Eucharist service they first gave thanks over the wine and then over the bread, then, following the conclusion of the meal, gave thanks to God together for: (1) the enjoyment of the food, (2) for the fellowship of friends, and (3) for the blessing which God had granted to them. They concluded, as stated by the text, remembering not Jerusalem, which would have been typical in a gathering of Jews at that time, but instead remembering the Church and making it a symbol of deliverance from evil. This shift marks a different understanding that has persisted over the centuries and will likely persist well into the future. Nevertheless, we can still affirm that the origin of the Eucharist had its foundation stone in the Jewish text. The Prayer for Jerusalem in the Birkat Ha-Mazon was composed during the battle of the Maccabees when the Temple and the Altar were under the control of pagans. From the connection between the oldest form of the Amidah and Sirach, we can infer that the prayer was composed between the time of Sirach and the Book of Jubilees. Therefore, one may conclude that in the study of the Didache we have evidence of the Jewish foundation of how the Eucharist came to become part of the liturgical supper and laid the foundation stone for the ritual and tradition of the early Church.

4)   **Jewish origins of the Last Supper**

With the discovery of the Dead Sea Scrolls, new insights into the origins of the sacrament of the Eucharist have materialized. The question following these discoveries revolves around the place the Essenes may have had in the rite? To put it succinctly, did the rite of the Eucharist also come from the Essenes?

When we read Josephus we note that," *before their meal, the Essenes purified themselves in cold water and after this purification, assembled in a private apartment that none of the uninitiated were permitted to enter. Upon purifying themselves, they repaired to the dining room, as if to some sacred shrine"*. This fragment of evidence provides us possible clues to the association of the Christian sacrament with the Essenes. The question may then be posed, was Jesus' last supper in Jerusalem also an Essene ceremony?

The fact that Jesus' last supper was celebrated during the Passover, leads us to believe that it was some form of a Passover ritual. Partaking of bread and wine, especially unleavened bread, was the most important part of the Passover meal. Typically, the feast day benediction came first. It began over a cup of wine, while the unleavened bread was kept covered. After the benediction, the cover over the bread was lifted and a benediction said for the bread. Why was the bread covered before the benediction was said over it? In the Jewish tradition, there was a symbolic rivalry between the wine and the bread. A cup of wine is considered better suited for the benediction of the feast, nevertheless the importance of the bread as the basis of the meal is undisputed. To resolve the problem, the bread was brought in on a small covered movable table before the Kaddish blessing of the wine was said.

The Essenes offered another solution for the rivalry between wine and bread; they always began with the benediction over the bread at the meal, and then the blessing over the wine. *"When they arranged the table for eating or the wine for drinking, the priest shall first stretch out his hand in order to bless the bread and the wine",* are the words directly taken from the Manual of Discipline, VI 4-6. The same will also happen at the Messianic Banquet in the last days. It will be forbidden that ***"a man shall stretch out his hand on the bread and the wine, before the priest, because the priest will bless the bread, and then the wine, and he will stretch out his hand on the bread at the beginning."*** So was the order of the Essene meal, which was firmly established regarding the bread and wine in contrast to the common Jewish custom when the wine comes distinctly before the bread. The orthodox way blesses the wine with the Kaddish prayer, then a blessing is made over the bread, the Challah prayer. What was uncovered with the Dead Sea Scrolls points out that the Essenes followed another tradition.

The question remains; did Jesus follow the Essene order in his festival meals, and especially the Last Supper, or did he follow an orthodox order, wine and then bread? What is important here is to uncover if the church established a new order or if it simply used the other order as practiced by the Essenes?.

According to Matthew and Mark, Jesus first blessed the bread and then the cup, a typical order of the Essene custom. The situation in Luke is different. *"And when the hour came, He sat at table and the Apostles with him, and he said to them, **'I have earnestly desired to eat this Passover with you before I suffer; for I tell you I shall not eat it until a new one shall be eaten in the kingdom of God.'** And he took a cup, and when he had given thanks he said **'take this and divide it amongst yourselves; for I tell you from now on I shall not drink of the fruit of the vine until the Kingdom of God comes.'** And he took the bread* *and when he had given thanks he broke it for them, saying,* ***'this is my body, take this in remembrance of me.'"*** (Luke 22:15-20) That ends the Luke text and so we note a different version from Matthew and Mark. Luke's original words about the Last Supper are consistent and clear enough. The question of whether both Luke and Mark base their accounts on two different oral traditions or whether the Matthew version is a re-written text based on an earlier source similar to the version of Luke, is the question that still remains to be answered.

My view is that perhaps Jesus was influenced by the Essene tradition. When he came to celebrate the Passover with his disciples, he followed the Essene practice and blessed the bread before the wine. It is interesting to note that Christian communities celebrate their communal meal in the same order as Jesus did, as non-sectarian Jews did with the bread preceding the wine. But what brought about the two ritual orders? Was it that the Essene tradition became part of the mother church of Jerusalem where Baptism became obligatory and a community of converts introduced. It is not possible to know exactly how communal meals were observed in Palestinian communities. We only know from the Act of the Apostles that day by day, they attended the Temple together and then broke bread in their homes, *"they partook with glad and generous hearts."* It is possible that this means that the bread was considered more essential; that it was necessary to partake of the bread to satisfy their hunger first and then the wine to signify their joy of communion.

While we do not know about the form of the Eucharist in the mother church in Palestine, both the form and the meaning of Holy Communion in Hellenistic churches in Paul's time are well known. These churches were influenced of the Essenes, not only in institutional ways, but also in their doctrinal teachings. We see it in

Paul's teaching in Corinthians 11:23-36. Paul practiced both the Essene order of first bread and then wine, as well as the form of the Last Supper as reflected in Luke. Paul evidently, in his pre-Christian life, used the Kaddish as the Pharisees did, with the bread following the blessing of the wine. He was comfortable with the order of the Last Supper. He therefore deemed the Eucharist cup to be the same wine the Jews drank after the grace was recited and the meal concluded. This cup, offered before the meal, is preceded by a benediction. Such considerations are reflected in Paul's words about the Last Supper. Paul found it necessary to stress that Jesus said the words, *"This cup is the new covenant in my blood"* after supper. For Paul, the solution to the order of the traditional meal was the fact that Jesus followed the reform minded Essene practices, pointing to his forthcoming passion, after the bread was consumed. The text of Luke reflects this practice.

In the early Hellenistic churches, not only was the Essene order of bread and wine introduced, but also the Essene theology that linked the concept of Christ's expiatory death with that of a new covenant. The importance of this idea in the Dead Sea Scrolls is well known. The word covenant never occurs in the mouth of Jesus in the Gospels, with the exception of the passage about the Last Supper in Mark 14:24 "this is my blood of the covenant which is poured out for the many." It also appears in Matthew 26:28 and the text of Luke 22:20. The sublime idea of the expiatory power of Christ's blood, which is the blood of the covenant, is concretized in the Eucharist where the wine becomes Jesus' blood. This concept became, according to the new tradition, a part of Jesus' words in the Last Supper as reflected in Mark and Luke and in I Corinthians 11:23-26. We have seen that in the original text of Luke, wine preceded the bread. This is the common Jewish order of benediction and was also likely

18

Jesus' practice. Later on, in many Christian communities, the order was reversed under the influence of the Essene communal meals, and it is clear that the reversed order stressed the sacramental character of the Eucharist because it seems that already the Essene common meal had become a sacred connection. It is impossible to know how the breaking of bread in the mother church took place, but in churches that Paul visited, the Essene practice of bread before wine was firmly established when he initially came into contact with them. In Hellenistic churches, the Essene order of the concept of the covenant of the community was linked with the idea of Christ's expiatory death and put into the mouth of Jesus himself.

The new order, and this new meaning of the Eucharist, was introduced by Mark in the Gospels and accepted by Matthew, later to be accepted by most of the churches. But it is significant that in the Didache (9-10), not only is the normal Jewish order of benediction wine, bread and then grace after meals preserved but also the concept of covenant is lacking. Thus, the question about the Essene influence on the Last Supper can be answered with the help of our new knowledge of both the normative and Essene style of Judaism.

We learn from the Luke text that in his meal, Jesus behaved as a orthodox Jew. In his Last Supper he both expressed the hope for the future and hinted at his imminent tragic death. Later, the Christian communal meal came under the Essene influence, with the Eucharist practiced to this day according to the tradition of the Essenes, first blessing the bread and then later the wine.

5) The Liturgical foundations of the early church and Synagogue

I came to study Christian Liturgy through my years at the University of Notre Dame where I was privileged to sing in the Notre Dame Glee Club during my college stay. There I began to notice the similarities not only in the Liturgy but in the music of both the synagogue and the church. I found many source materials as I studied both the Christian text and the Hebrew text. Here are some of the parallels which I discovered.

CHRISTIAN TEXT	**HEBREW TEXT**
1.Oh thou holy God will you seek wisdom and teach us understanding?	1.Thou favourest man, teach us with knowledge and good understanding.
2.Elect a God oh happy and blessed priest. Liken unto Aaron and the Prophet Moses	2.He made excellent Aaron; he adorned him in glory.
3.It is meek and right	3.It is meek and right
4.Holy, Holy, Holy is the Lord of Hosts; full of His glory are the heavens and the earth.	4.Holy, Holy, Holy is the Lord of of Hosts; full of his glory is the earth.
5.We pray for peace and God's benevolence and for the salvation of our souls.	5.He who makes peace in his heavens, may he make peace for us and for all the world.
6.Have mercy upon us, Oh God, ruler of all men!	6.Our Father, our King, have mercy upon us!
7.May he implant them the salutary fear of the Lord.	7.May he implant in them the fear of the Lord.
8.Arise to God, bow to Him and praise Him.	8.Arise and bless the Lord to whom all praise is due.
9.Gather together thy church from the corners of the earth unto thy Kingdom.	9.Gather us from the four corners of the earth.
10.Praise be thou forever and ever, shield of Abraham.	10.Praise be thou Oh Lord of the Universe, shield of Abraham.

11.Praise be thou, King of the Universe, who through Christ has created, and through Him has ordered the cayotic.

11.Praise be thou oh Lord who forms light and causes darkness, makes peace and creates all things.

12.Thou has abolished death. Thou who givest life to the dead.

12.Faithful art thou to quicken the dead. Praise art thou Oh Lord who quickens the dead.

13.And the host of angels, fiery and ardent proclaim, one is Holy.

13.One holy said to another unknown, we shall revere and sanctify thee according to the mystic utterance.

14.For thou art the Father of wisdom, the giver of law.

14.Thou favourest man with knowledge and give us the law.

15.For the Sabbath is rest and from creation, the gold of the universe the study of the law.

15.For the Sabbath is rest from creation given to the study of the law.

16.And thou hast mercy upon Zion and rebuilt Jerusalem and directed in its midst the throne of David

16.And to Jerusalem, the city, return in mercy and rebuild it soon in our days and set up the throne of David.

17.We give thanks to thee oh king for everything in the days of Esther and Mortichai.

17.We give thanks unto thee oh God for the days of Mortichai and Esther.

18.Above all we glorify and praise thee now and forever, Amen

18.For all that thy name, oh King, shall be blessed and exalted forever.

19.Do not reject us unto the end for the sake of thy holy name and do not break your covenant .

19.Oh Lord, let not wrath rule over us we beseech thee give heed to the covenant with Abraham my friend.

20.A whole lifetime and many centuries would not surface for us to praise thee as becomes thy dignity.

20.Though our mouths were full of song as the sea and our tongues full of exaltation, we should still be able to thank thee and praise thy name.

21.God without beginning, without ending.

21.God without beginning, without ending.

22.Gather him in the realm of the
the great ones who rest with
Abraham, Isaac and Jacob.

22.Shelter him among the holy and
pure with Abraham, Isaac and
Jacob.

23.Save thy people and bless
 thine inheritance, thou hast
assumed.

23.Help thy people and bless
thy Heritage among us.

24.Guard us under the protection
of thy wings, Oh our God and
keep away from us everything
evil and hostile
.

24.Shelter us under the shadow of
thy wings, remove also the
adversary from before us and from
behind us.

25.Praise be thou oh kingdom,
oh father, for the Son, and Holy
Spirit, now and forevermore
unto eternity without end.

25.Blessed be his name, his
glorious kingdom is forever and
ever.

26.Sing a song to our God and
spiritual songs in a sweet
voice of melody.

26.For unto thee, Oh Lord our
God, songs are becoming
hymns and Psalm, blessing
and thanksgiving.

27.Oh living God, rule thou oh
Lord; adorned for it is worthy
and true, with our just and
need and greatness of thy
holiness.

27.Oh King, Lord our God,
such is the duty of all creation
in thy presence to thank,,praise
and glorify thy name.

28.Oh Lord our God,
compassionate, and merciful
long suffering and plentiness
in mercy, give ear to our
prayer and attend to the voice
of our entreaty.

28.Oh God, hear our prayers and
deliver us from all trouble, for
thee alone, Oh God, do we find
our strength.

29.Bestow, Oh Lord in your
loving kindness and salvation
unto the oppressed. Release
to the prisoner.

29.As for our brethren, each
such of them as are given
over to trouble, or captivity
may the all present have mercy
upon them.

CHAPTER TWO
Parallels between the Synagogue and the early Church

1) Use of the Psalms for worship in Church and Synagogue

The book of Psalms contains almost every great religious idea that grew up in Israel. Some of the Psalms are epic poetry of a type, as exampled by the song of Debra, found in Psalms 18. There are Psalms, which express the ethical idealism of the prophets. Some Psalms express the mood of study and the love of wisdom, characteristic of the Book of Proverbs. Other Psalms echo the great historical vision of the roll of God as the guide to human destiny as expressed in Deuteronomy and in the historic books. The Book of the Psalms is an epitome of all the noble religious ideas developed in Israel.

Beside the Psalms embodying ideas of Biblical literature, they also posses a uniqueness of mood and expression; a spirit, which was bound to give them, a universal appeal. Although many Psalms were often understood as describing the vicissitudes of the whole people of Israel, there are others that express a personal mood. They describe the inner life, tenderly and vividly. Through pure lyrical poetry, they describe emotional aspect of the spiritual life. In this regard, the Psalms are unique in literature. The book of Psalms contains the whole music of the heart of man swept by the hand of his Maker. In these are gathered the lyrical burst of tenderness, the moan of pentenance, the groan of sorrow, the triumph of victory, the despair of defeat, the firmness of human confidence, and the rapture of assured hope. In these are presented the anatomy of all the parts of the human soul. As the poet Heine says, *"The sunrise and sunset, birth and*

death, promise and fulfillment. The whole drama of
humanity is recorded in the Psalms."

The literature of antiquity was rich in many types
of expressions but it was purest in voicing the language of
the heart. The Hebrew Psalms were the first to give
expression to the conversation of the human heart with
God, uttered in pure lyric language, before it was uttered by
any other literary source. David, is the first of the poets in
the feeling mood, considered the King of Lyrics. Never has
the thought of a poet risen so high and so pure, never has
the soul opened before man and God in language so tender,
so sympathetic, so moving as was voiced by King David.
All the secret cries of the human heart found a voice
through his life. It is not surprising, therefore, that the Book
of Psalms is the most widely read of all the Biblical books.

It was largely due to the Psalms that the Bible
became one of the most influential books in the world.
When Christians emerged from Palestine and began to
spread westward, the book of Psalms was their hymnbook
and all the Old Testament books, their greatest inspiration.
The early church made constant use of it. *"It was the first*
book which the early church put into the hands of her young
converts. The primer of her religious teachings, and no man
could be admitted to the highest order of the clergy unless he
knew the Psalms by heart. It was used for singing in the
first assemblies of Christian worship and it has ever since
continued to be used, sometimes as the sole book of praise,
but always as the best and most enduring of all." (Taken
from a book by Dr. James Robertson, in his study of the
Psalms and Christian worship).

When the New Testament was published apart from
the Old, the Book of Psalms was printed with it. It was
used as frequently as the Gospel itself. In many
denominations, the Psalms are printed together with the
prayer book. There is hardly a festival or Saint's day that

does not have a specific Psalm assigned to it. Not only has the Psalm book officially been used by the church since the beginning of Christianity, its influence on the personal life of its leaders is still a driving force in the spiritual life of many of the clergy.

In the Catholic Church the daily office of the religious, whether priests, brothers or nuns- all have a Book of Psalms as their basic prayer book. In the life and thought of the Jewish people, the Psalms have continually exerted a profound influence. The influence of the Psalms is conspicuous in the development of the prayer book. The Jewish Prayer Book, the first text for purely spiritual worship in the history of religion, is almost an echo of the Book of Psalms itself. In the earliest religious service, the Torah and the Prophets were read and interpreted for the purpose of instruction. But the spiritual and emotional parts of the service, that which became the actual text of the prayer book itself, came almost entirely from the Book of Psalms.

Many of the Psalms were simply embodied in the service and perhaps the bulk of the original content of the service. To this day the regular synagogue service consists largely of Psalms or partial Psalm verses. In the daily service, Psalms 145-150 are read for every Jewish Holiday, Sabbath, and festival and a special Psalm for each day. The Jewish prayer book holds together as long as the Psalms bring it together in its various moods, which themselves bring spirit, hope and the faith of Israel in its longing for God and its search for spiritual serenity.

When we study the earliest liturgy of the early church and synagogue we can't help but notice how similar the use of Psalms is evidenced in both services. For example, Psalm 100 opens both the Catholic Mass and the synagogue service with these words. *"Make a joyful noise unto the Lord all ye lands. Serve the Lord with gladness.*

*Come before his presence with singing. Know ye that the
Lord is God and we are his people. Enter into his gates with
thanksgiving and into his courts with praise."* How
beautiful it is that both Synagogue and Mass use the words
of the Psalms. The Church not only uses the words, they
have also used the melodies that came from the older
tradition.

Recently the great, late scholar and my dear teacher,
Dr. Eric Werner, traced the fact that the Gregorian chant
used by the Catholic church and the traditional chant of the
Greek and Russian Orthodox church, are each based on the
cantilation of the Torah, the first five books of Moses.
Jewish tradition developed a certain melodic chant to chant
the words of the Torah to better preserve the ancient
tradition. It's interesting to note that while the early church
broke with the synagogue, theologically, it maintained the
same liturgical and musical tradition   When we examine, for
example, the morning service, we note that Psalms 145 is
used for both synagogue and church. The same words and
tones can be heard in Hebrew, Latin, English or Greek: *"I
will extol thee Oh my God and King, I will bless thy name
forever and ever. Everyday will I bless thee and I will
praise thy name forever. Great is the Lord and highly to be
praised and his greatness is unsearchable. One generation
shall praise thy works to another and shall declare thy
mighty acts."* The hope and prayer of both Jew and
Christian is rooted in that Psalm in which the praise of God
lifts the spirit of the people. Both Jews and Christians have
carried on a near identical tradition unknowingly when they
both read and sang the Psalms in an identical fashion.

The first form of singing Psalms was by a soloist
who would chant the Psalms at the beginning of the service.
We find this both in the synagogue where the cantor begins
the Sabbath service with the 92nd Psalm. *"How good it is
to thank the Lord, to praise thy name, oh thou most high."*

If one studies the opening of the Catholic Mass, one is struck by the fact that the very same Psalm is used, and usually it is the priest conducting the Mass who will begin by chanting this Psalm. In the past, it was the Gregorian chant whose melodies were heard, today other melodies are used by the church.

The second form of Psalm chanting, in both the Jewish and Christian liturgy, began to develop in choral psalm singing in the church. This practice offered a powerful stimulus for the Monastic rule, finally resulting in the creation of a new form of music called antiphonal. It should be kept in mind that the term had a two fold or even a three-fold meaning before the fifth century. As antiphonal singing, it designated alternative singing of two choruses. That was the ancient Jewish practice as known in the Hebrew Bible, especially as it was presented in Second Chronicles 20:19-21 *"And they stood up to praise the Lord God of Israel with a loud voice on high... And they rose early in the morning, and went forth into the wilderness... and as they went forth, Jehoshaphat stood and said, Hear me and ye inhabitants of Jerusalem; Believe in the Lord your God, so shall ye be established; believe his prophets, so shall ye prosper. And when he had consulted with the people, he appointed singers unto the Lord, that should praise the beauty of holiness, as they went out before the army, and to say, Praise the Lord; for his mercy endureth forever."* Thus, the use of two choruses was well known during the Temple days and we find it also in Psalms 136: *"Oh give thanks unto the Lord; for he is good; for his mercy endureth forever."*

During the third and fourth century, this way of singing became popular in the church. It became the tradition of the Monasteries, that there would be two choruses to sing the songs. One chorus would began and the second chorus would respond. This antiphonal musical

27

form became the standard approach in many churches and is still done today. Recently, the church uncovered historic proof that the early Jewish pilgrims, celebrating the high holy days, would stand before the great door of the Temple and sing to the priests on the other side of the door. Each would sing to the other, until the great door was opened to the waiting pilgrims. After the destruction of the great Temple, the synagogue did not expand its Psalm singing as the church would do. The practice of the lone cantor, being totally in charge without choir or without the stimulation of choral singing, became the musical voice of the synagogue. Within the church, choral singing became an important part of the liturgy.

Today, in various Monasteries and Convents the singing of Psalms has become a way of life, to the point that in the church, one part of the church represents one part of the choral voice, while the second part of the church represents the second choral voice. One begins: the other responds. In the recent discovery of the Dead Sea Scrolls we also find that the Essenes living by the Dead Sea used this form of singing in their morning worship service. They had their own Psalms and hymns, which they sang in an antiphonal manner. The manuscripts show where one chorus would begin and the other chorus would respond. Thus, we have a most interesting picture of the same kind of singing the great Jewish philosopher from Alexandria, Philo, explained in his description of a Jewish sect, called the "Therpeulie of Egypt," that existed during the first century: *"They arise from both sides, forming two choirs, one of men, the other of woman - then they sing hymns to God in various meters and tunes, sometimes altogether, sometimes alternately. Later they combine the two choruses into one chorus like the Jewish people did when they went through the Red Sea."* Such singing of the faithful reminds us of what was done by the priests and pilgrims in the

Temple.

The third form of repeating the Psalms was what we know now as responsive reading. There the leader recites one verse and the congregation responds with the next verse. That is still continued today, both in Protestant, Catholic and Jewish houses of worship. We read Psalms today usually during the responsive reading of the congregation. This mode came from the Temple, for the Psalms of the Temple were lead by the High Priest who would read the first line, while the congregation would voice an appropriate response. The Psalms are sung, chanted and spoken in many languages and lands even today.

One of the oldest churches in Christianity, the Armenian Church, follows more closely the Jewish Traditional service than does the Eastern Orthodox or the Roman Catholic. If one studies the Armenian prayer book, one finds the reminiscences of the three Jewish services for Sabbath- morning, afternoon and evening.

For the morning service, Psalms 145 to 150 are at the beginning of the Sabbath service and the same is found to be true for the Armenian Church. In the afternoon service Psalms are used but chanted in the Armenian language. The Armenian Church has adopted the use of the Hallel, which occurs in the Armenian ritual in the same way in which the synagogue uses these Psalms. *"Oh give thanks unto the Lord for He is good and His mercy endureth forever".* In addition to the Armenia Service beginning its service with the same Psalms as offered in the Synagogue, the responsive readings of Psalms 148 to 150 during the service are the same.

It's fascinating how the Armenians adopted the Jewish Liturgy and yet were not aware of this similarity until recently. At a recent gathering of the National Conference of Christians and Jews held in Jerusalem, the Armenians were represented. During an initial session the

Armenian priests suddenly recognized that the Jewish Liturgy they were studying was identical to the one they had used, for the passed two thousand years. The only difference appeared to be the days the Psalms were employed. The Psalms, which Jews sang on Saturday, Armenians sang on Sunday.

We note the interesting parallels in the Greek and Russian Orthodox liturgy. For example, the Greek Orthodox church uses the Psalms in the beginning of their services, dividing the Psalms into three categories, the identical way that the Synagogue divides them. The order is as follows: First, Thanksgiving, second, praise, and third, the use of the hallelujah Psalms. One observes that they use two choruses instead of one. The priest chants the first line and the congregation responds with the second line. In this, they follow what the Synagogue did centuries ago and what the Temple practiced even before the Synagogue. There are fragments of evidence that support the path the Psalms took from the Temple to the Synagogue to the Greek Orthodox and Russian Orthodox churches. To this day, the same Psalms are heard sung in contemporary Orthodox services, except that they are sung in Greek or Russian. It is evident that chanting of Psalms has become a way of life that is still practiced today.

The Greek Orthodox Church has uniquely developed antiphonal singing between two singular choruses for special holidays and celebrations. The Roman Catholic Church uses the Book of Psalms to that same degree. The psalms have become the single most important part of their liturgy. The regular use of Psalms in all liturgical settings provide clear evidence of their importance in the worship experience of Catholicism. Special Psalms have been assigned to be sung or chanted on most occasions throughout the liturgical calendar year, proof of Judaism's place in the religion that sprang from its loins. .

In Judaism, the regular rendering of Psalms served two purposes:

(1) A memorial of the Temple, as demanded by the rabbis, and

(2) As a fulfillment of the divine command: *"You shall love the Lord your God with all your heart and all your soul by daily praise and laudation"*.

Less we forget, the Hebrew term for Psalms is Sefer tehillin, or the Book of Praise. The latter function examples Paul's demand for members of the early churches he visited to follow the prayer service of the Temple, a service heavily imbued with Psalms. While Paul acknowledged an early church that had broken with the Synagogue, he insisted the psalms remain a part of the new worship.

During Passover, we use certain Psalms in the Aggadah. The early morning service uses them as well. The Hallel, begins with the words of Psalm 118: *"Oh give thanks to the Lord for He is good and His mercy endureth forever"*. The church employs the same Psalm on both Good Friday and the following Holy Saturday. On Easter Sunday the hallelujah Psalm, which ends the Book of Psalms, is used at the conclusion of the Easter service. The Hallelujah is also recited at the Passover Seder in which Jews commemorate the going forth of the people of God from Egypt. There too, Psalms are recited at the Seder table.

Psalm 118 takes first place at both the Passover and Easter Services. It is both the Easter and Passover Psalm par excellence. It has always been sung during Holy Week and the following Easter Sunday. The Jewish celebration of Passover also uses Psalm 114, a Psalm that has found its place on Easter Sunday. It appears to be an interesting historic fact that the early church fathers, who made up the Liturgy for Easter week, adapted the same Psalms used

31

during Rosh Hashanah, the Jewish New Year, and Yom Kippur, the holiest day of the Jewish calendar year. Their regular usage corresponds to Easter Sunday, the holiest day of the Church.year.

The following Psalms were chanted during Holy Week: Psalms 51, 67, 92 and 150. They were also inserted in Synagogue services to mark penitential themes. Many of those Psalms chanted in church, conclude with the Psalm of Hallelujah. This theme has become the universal anthem for both Judaism and Christianity. It could be argued that the church reached its pinnacle of spontaneous prayer in the fourth century when it used the Psalms antiphonally., as the temple had done centuries before. A later synagogue would develop its own Psalter type singing, but in contrast to its earlier period, it would do so through use of a cantor and congregational responses.

What is so beautiful to consider is that both church and synagogue had the same prayer book; the only difference being in the use of different Psalms on different occasions and for different holidays. The words were the same. They both followed a old tradition, which even to this day is an important rock upon which the spiritual heritage of both the church and the synagogue are integrally related. We are all children of one God and we have enjoyed a common prayer book; namely,the Book of Psalms, dear to the hearts of both faiths. It is the universal character of these Psalms that made it the prayer book of Protestants, Catholics and Jews. Thus, the Psalms became a spiritual ladder, which united the one God with all his children. We who are heirs to this great legacy must continue to study how each of us use the Psalms and how each of us make the Psalms a way of life through a way of prayer. They have built for us the spiritual ladder by which we can ascend the mountain of the Lord and there praise his Holy name. Reciting the Psalms, makes us one people with one God, and one covenant.

2).   **The Aesthetic of the Liturgy in**
       the early Church and Synagogue

Pope Pious 11th proclaimed to the world:
"spiritually, we are all Semites". In this statement, the late
pope was able to understand the Aesthetic and spiritual
values of the music through the Liturgy of both the
synagogue and the early church. In Biblical literature, the
idea that music is simply beautiful, is of no meaning. In the
synagogue and in the Temple music had it place, as part of
the ritual and liturgy of the Temple. It was central but not
independent, an accompaniment of the prayer service.

It is interesting to note the difference between the
Greek view of life and that of the Hebrew. The Greek
tradition stood rooted in the idea of the beautiful against the
ugly. The Hebraic tradition was based on the holy verses
the profane. To the Jewish singer, chanting the Psalms was
to be a holy experience, although it could incidentally be
beautiful. This became part of the tradition that the early
church inherited from the synagogue.

As the Greek Philosopher looked to the beautiful,
the Jewish Philosopher looked to the holy and the sacred.
We remember a story in the Talmud of Rabbi Joshua Ben
Hananya who made this remark: *"Rabbi Hananya was an
ugly hunchback. Once a king's daughter ridiculed him for
being ugly and marveled, rather dubiously, that a treasury
of wisdom should be sheltered in so unattractive an abode.
Whereupon, Rabbi Joshua asked her, in what kind of
vessels they preserve their best wines; in silver, in gold or
in clay. She informed him that the best wines are kept in
simple clay containers. He then asked her why it should
surprise her that the beauty of learning and wisdom would
be sheltered in so physically unattractive a person as the
one who stood before her."*

Socrates, too was unseemly in appearance but incredible in intellectual reasoning. Like Rabbi Joshua, he exampled the truth that wisdom can be applied from a physically ugly person.

We know from the Bible, that the Temple used many musical instruments in religious services. At the dedication of King Solomon's Temple there were a thousand musicians and singers in the service. Consequently, we can say that instrumental music played an important part in the music and liturgy of the Temple.

The most important thing was that vocal music was considered to be on a higher plain than instrumental music. We know that in Judaism, as well as in early Christianity, the primacy of vocal over instrumental performances seemed so firmly established, it became a way of life for both synagogue and early church to prefer vocal music over instrumental. With the destruction of the second Temple, instrumental music was not allowed in the synagogue: the people were in mourning over the loss of their Temple. From the beginning, it was understood that vocalized liturgy was the most primary form of music in the synagogue. The interesting part of this tradition is that the early church also emphasized the vocal tradition.

Cyprian, bishop of Carthage, the same who pronounced that outside the church there is no salvation, banished the playing of instrumental music in the church. He said: *"The fact that David danced before God is no excuse for those Christians who sit in the theater - for them harps, cymbals, flutes and other instruments, are not sounded for the Glory of God, but for idols. Through the scheme of the devil, holy instruments have become illicit."*

The early church realized from their scriptures that Judaism had brought instrumental music into the tradition of the liturgy, but they looked negatively upon that practice. They spoke of using instruments as identical to becoming Judaized, and even such church fathers as John Chrysostom condemned it's use. In the Middle Ages, this argument had so staunch a champion as St. Thomas Aquinas, who opposed the organ because he thought it might jade the church. The fact was, the synagogue had no instrumental music. However, this was unknown to early church fathers, whose extreme psychological hostility to the traditions of the synagogue surfaced in many of their writings, even while they were uninformed.

We now realize that the early church's attitude towards instrumental music was influenced by the fact that it was determined to rid its ranks of all foreign/pagan influences. The church felt itself engaged in a spiritual battle with all of the pagan influences, and that included instrumental music. The earlier Jewish tradition of employing instrumental music was lumped together with the pagan practices whose rituals included instrumental music. But from the time of the synagogue onward, the Jews had banished instrumental music from their services. The synagogue chose to banish that musical expression because it wanted to symbolically remember the destruction of the Temple. The church chose to banish that expression because it felt threatened by foreign modes of attractive communication. Today, most church services employ instrumental music and consider it to be essential to a normal service. It's fascinating to realize that both church and synagogue chose to institute the same practice without the one realizing what the other was doing. It's also interesting to remember that each harbored a totally different reason for their corporate decision.

After the destruction of the Temple, vocal music became the primary source of music for the synagogue. It was used in chanting the prayers as well singing the daily Psalms in the morning service, a remnant of the former Temple ritual. The Psalms were simple and uniform for leading the people to sing praises to God with on's heart and soul. A careful distinction was also made between different types of Psalm singing. There was antiphonal singing with the cantor leading the congregation, as well as responsive reading by congregation and cantor.

This concept of congregational participation became part of the New Testament liturgy of the early church. We note that the early church used the Psalms in the same way; in fact they sang the same songs. The early Christians made vocal tradition the center of their musical spirit. They rarely used instrumental music. That came later. The early church fathers were much concerned that the church should follow the tradition of vocal music. It is interesting to note that Justin Martyr had by then traced the origin of the Christian song back to a declaration made by Jesus himself, while Pope's Damasus and Celestine seemed to associate the chants of the church with the tradition of the synagogue. There was conflict in the early church, as some opposed this kind of singing. They felt that nothing should be adopted from the synagogue. Their feelings exampled a growing Anti-Semitic sentiment. Those sentiments further reflected in their rejection of chanting in the church.

The argument raised by some of the early church fathers denoted a misplacement of priorities. It went something like this: If the Jews sang in their services because this would loosen their hardened hearts and infidels use music to seduce men in their thinking, why should the church follow this practice? The church neither seduces men nor is hard of heart. The answer, these fathers posited, lies in the argument that: singing itself, condemnable on the basis of simple-mindedness, leads to the accompaniment of heartless instruments, dance and the rattling of drums, all of which disturb the spirit of the service. Yet, to be fair, there were differences of opinion. St. Jerome advised his contemporaries that he wanted to chant the Psalms in

Hebrew. Thus, he introduced some Hebrew into the early Christian liturgy by chanting the Psalms in their original language, a practice the synagogue is still doing,

Early church Fathers like St. Ambrose and St. Augustine made a distinction between their vocal music and that of the Jews. Observe what St. Ambrose had to say: *"The hymns and the Psalms should be to us, a manifestation of God. Thus, the Lord's Testament is called Canticle, because we sing the remission of all sinners and the just acts of the Lord in the Gospels, in sweet exaltation of our heart. The Lord himself did not disdain to say we have sung unto you and you have not danced. He sang for us in the Gospels, forgiveness of sins; the Jew should apply themselves to it, not in histrionic gestures of the body, but spiritually. They have failed to do so; hence, they are to be condemned."*

From a theological point of view, it should be noted from his last statement that he didn't object to music sung to the glory of God, but to copying what he considered <u>unsaved</u> musical practices. That it is an open contradiction to the apostle Paul, who believed that there should be use of vocal music in the synagogue service and newly created church services. The difference lies in the fact that Paul was of Jewish descent while Ambrose and Augustine were of gentile descent. *"Ten strings unknown as the psalter and Ten Commandments of the law. To sing and chant is usually the occupation of loving men. The old man is in fear, the new one in love. Thus, do we discern two Testaments, the old, and the new love then sings the new song - even the old man could have a psalter of ten strings, for the Jews in the flesh, the law of the Ten Commandments was given; but he who lives in the law cannot sing the new song, for he stands under the law and yet cannot fulfill it. He possess the organ, but does not use it."* These words of Ambrose are mild compared with Chrysostrom's thundering tirade against the *"vile, stubborn, treacherous, and despicable Jews."* But even this tirade can be understood by a fair minded and historically sensitive person, if one takes into account the pent up emotions which the conflict of church and synagogue has engendered over the centuries.

Another consideration are women and liturgy. What was the position of women in the liturgical chanting of the service? Paul issued a rule that went like this: *"The women shall be silent in the assemblies."* This referred to their singing. In strict informaty with the Rabbinic practice of the synagogue, women were not allowed to sing. Later the church would change its opinion on women as promoted by Paul. It was, in fact, St. Ambrose who championed women singing in the services. He links his remarks to Paul's injunction, and merit quoting when he says *"The Apostles command the women to be silent in church, yet they sing well the Psalms, for the Psalms are sweet and appropriate to every age and every sex; here the old ones abolish the sternness of their age, the sorry elderly men respond joyfully, the young men sing it but the women truly love it. Thus, the women chant so beautifully that their voices should be heard."*

The reason the synagogue opposed the use of women's voices was because it felt that female participation would lead to licentiousness. Jewish Heretics unscrupulously used female choirs as a way to promote popular attractions not in keeping with strict worship. In conclusion, as we survey the parallels between the synagogue and the early church, it is obvious they both had the same vocal traditions. Unfortunately, they developed hostility and anger toward one another. Yet, when it came to singing the Psalms, they were chanting the same words and practically the same music. The church finally adopted many of the melodies of the synagogue. It considered them sacred from Temple times. As the early Christians looked

upon themselves as the new Israel, they ultimately
championed the vocal music of the synagogue and made it
part of their own tradition.

3)   **Parallels in the Liturgy of the Synagogue
and the early Church**

The first Christians were Jews, both by faith and
nationality. Their ritual was the Jewish cult. Their language
was Hebrew and Aramaic. While they accepted the Jewish
institutions of their time, they expanded and reinterpreted
them to be in keeping with their new message of salvation.
They obviously carried the background and heritage of their
past with them. They were Jews in terms of their faith,
education and training.

At the time of the birth of Christianity, there were
three forms of Jewish worship, all well established during
Jesus' lifetime. Jews found their worship expression
through these three different media:
(1) in the sacrificial cult of the Temple in Jerusalem, the
central sanctuary of the country;
(2) in the services of many of the local synagogues, Jesus
attended; and
(3) in private devotion, a part of family tradition.
All three were very important in both the life of Jesus and
of his disciples.

When the Temple was destroyed in the year 70, the
Christian religion began to separate itself almost completely
from the synagogue. We have this fact illustrated by
historic evidence that they were no longer friends with each
other. Regardless of the hostility that existed between
church and synagogue the church Fathers emphasize the
Temple as the model to be imitated by the Church.
Comparisons frequently stress a type of hierarchy common
to church and Temple. Jerome states: *"Aaron, his sons
and Levites, were in the Temple, the same Bishops, priests,*

and deacons are in the church." Indeed, the church hierarchy developed from the priestly organization of the Temple. Later it would modify itself to more closely copy the Roman system of government. In its early years the church followed the musical and liturgical elements of the synagogue, a reasonable result of the early church's acquaintance with synagogue practice. We have no complete record as to what was used and what was not used. We do know the church service followed the normal Sabbath morning service. The change from Saturday to Sunday came later. In the early days, it likely was part of worship to do so on Saturday, the traditional Sabbath day.

The most important part of the Christian cult, with regards to liturgy, is to understand that there was a bond between the liturgies of the synagogue, the Temple, and early Christian worship. We may then ask the question, what were the common elements in the worship of the early church that were common to the liturgies of the synagogue and the Temple. We learn primarily from the liturgical texts that most of the prayers originated in the Temple but were adapted by the early synagogue. Of course, there was the hierarchy of the high priest in the Temple and the Levites and other functionaries who worked in the Temple all of whom took part in the Temple ritual. We now know there were ceremonials and rituals, parts of the synagogue and Temple, which later became part of the church. The music of the church and its manner of performance must have had some relationship to both synagogue and Temple from the time they separated from the Jewish community. They must have carried on a tradition very similar to that of the traditional music they had known and passed on from previous generations. Continuity and holding traditions are essential factors for a religion that issues from another faith.

There is yet another factor, that directly relates to organization and observance of the ecclesiastical year. The

Jewish calendar had become a mixture of different elements coming from the tradition of the Jews when they had lived both in Babylon and Egypt. These historic periods carried certain traditions which were now part of an Ecclesiastical program. One of the interesting parts of the beginning of Christian liturgy was its sense of connectedness with the Temple tradition. It is interesting to note in the writings of Clement of Rome this statement he made to the Corinthians: *"That each of you, Brethren in his own order give thanks unto God, maintaining a good conscience and not transgressing the appointed rule of his service but acting with all good. Not in every place, Brethren are the commanded daily sacrifices offered, or the freewill offering, or sin offerings or the trespass offerings, but in Jerusalem alone. Even there the offering is not made in every place but before the sanctuary, in the court of the altar; and thus through the high priest and respective ministers."*

This passage is remarkable for several reasons: First, Clement of Rome was probably the third bishop of Rome. While it is assumed today that the Epistle from which we have just quoted was written between 95 and 100 CE, it is not clear how its author 26 years after the destruction of the Temple, could refer to the institution as still existing, a problem that has baffled leading theologians even to this day. Perhaps, Clement saw the temple as continuing even though it had ceased to be a liturgical center of the Jewish community. Yet, he had a sense of reverence for the Temple and the Temple liturgy. It was likely that Clement saw the church as the truth successor to the Temple, thus taking over the many functions, the Temple performed. We note that the very early church did have a reverence for the past. They felt that they were continuing traditions handed down to them by their predecessors. Thus, the early church continued a tradition of the Temple even though they may have forgotten many of the prayers or rituals. Yet, in their hearts they felt they were continuing a tradition that was sacred to them.

There was a distinct difference between Temple worship and synagogue worship.Temple worship centered in the sacrificial cult, executed by a highly trained staff of professional priests who held their privileged position through inheritance, as a birthright. At the time, you became a priest in the Temple sanctuary only if you were born to it. The synagogue, on the other hand, was the house of prayer, meditation and a most important place of study. In the Temple, the priesthood prevailed in all its ceremonial splendor. In the synagogue, it was the scholar and the layman who molded the service into a form, basically unchanged to this day. The Rabbi, or teacher, replaced the priest as the leader and teacher, bringing his congregation understanding of the faith through prayer and learning. The attitude of the Temple was essentially theocratic and ritualistic. The attitude of the synagogue was democratic in structure and people centered in its welcome.

Despite the basic differences between the two institutions of Temple and Synagogue, there was common ground. The closest link between them was the "Temple-synagogue," a synagogue established in the Hall of Stones in the Temple, referred to in the New Testament as Solomon's Hall. We know of this remarkable place of worship through Jewish and New Testament sources. It was identical with the hall in which Jesus debated with the rabbis, as mentioned in Luke 2:46, and later referenced in Acts 3:11, and 5:12. Here, prayers were spoken, meetings held, and readings of the law pronounced. Public discussions would also take place, but the space served chiefly as a gathering place for those devoted men who made this their special place of study and worship. Groups of 24 men took turns in the performance of ritual duties. Laymen had the privilege of standing by and witnessing the daily sacrifices in the Temple, but could not function as priests. Before the ceremony, they met the official priest in the Hall of Stones where, in the presence of the people, they received the blessing. After the sacrifice, these special men returned to the hall where they attended a service of their own. They were often referred to as "the standing men" since they stood together as one group. The participation of laymen from all parts of the country created a strong link between the central sanctuary and the synagogue. Thus, all the discussions that we read about in the New Testament regarding conversations between Jesus and the men of the Synagogue must have taken place in this Hall of Stones. The Hall of Stones also provided the link between the high priest and the spiritual leaders of the synagogue. When the Christian church began, of course, these traditions continued as long as the Temple stood. After 70 CE the synagogue replaced the sacrifices with recitation of certain prayers. The early church then saw the sacrifice of Jesus on the Roman cross as fulfilling sacrifice services and Temple worship.

When the great Temple was destroyed in 70 CE, Rabbi Johanan Zakkai established the academy of Jabne. The Academy assumed a fragment of the prerogative of the Temple. That fragment included the taxation of tithes, and the privilege of the Shoffer signals on the part of the priests and members of the priestly caste. It was also an historic fact that the Jabne began to develop prayers and responses, that became typical for all synagogues even to this day. Of the several personalities who endeavored to transfer the tradition of the central sanctuary to the country synagogue, none was as colorful and remarkable as Rabbi Joshua Ben Hanany, known both as a traditionalist and an adversary of early Christianity. A Levite priest, he lived in the second century. As a member of the division of singers, he had conducted daily worship in the Solomon Hall of Stone and officiated at both services. He was a personal disciple of Johanan Ben Zakkai and worked zealously for the preservation of the tradition of the Temple by faithfully transmitting it to the synagogue. Many of his statements bear out his attitude. A man of the world, a statesmen, dealing with emperor Hadrian, a witty debater and a wise and pious man, he tried his best to heal the breech between the Temple and the synagogue. At the same time, he was deeply troubled by the schism created by the birth of the early church. He incessantly opposed the split and denounced the early church as being heretical. Conceiving the early church to be a threat to the synagogue, he was negative towards the early Jewish Christians and their way of worship. Not afraid of Gentile Christianity, he was fearful of a Jewish Christianity. Thus, we see how the conflict began, with both sides becoming extremely defensive of their respective liturgies and positions in the Roman world.

Though the split was inevitable, common elements in the liturgy of Christianity and Judaism remained intact in substance, in form and in the manner of their performance. What were these common elements?

First, scriptural lesson reading, which in the course of time, developed into a highly organized system of readings throughout the church year and for various holidays.

Secondly, the field of chanting Psalms was an important part of both liturgies. After the church departed from the synagogue, it still continued to sing the Psalms recalling an earlier tradition, thus bringing the Psalms to become an integral part of the worship.

Thirdly, there were congregation prayers of supplication and intercession, especially on fast days, becoming a part of the calendar year for both church and synagogue.

Finally, there was the chanted prayer of the priest or the precentor. This came later, becoming an important element in the liturgy, predominate in the synagogue as well as in some rituals of the Eastern Church. In the Jewish tradition, the Cantor became the musical voice of the synagogue, while the priest in many ways became the musical voice of the church. To this very day, they constitute the very center of Liturgical music. We see how the early church and synagogue went on their different ways but really maintained a strong bond through liturgy and music. Though church and synagogue appear totally separate now and at times somewhat antagonistic to each other, the sacred bond of liturgy and music has held them together, expressing a basic faith from the beginning.

4) **Angels in Jewish and Christian Liturgies**

Angels have played a strong role in the writings of both the Hebrew Bible and the Christian Scriptures. In both, angels appear as superior to man in knowledge and power, but subornate to God. These beings served as God's attendants, like courtiers of an earthly king, serving as God's agents to convey messages to men; instructing them to carry out the will of the Almighty. It was inevitable that angels should also become part of the liturgy for both Christian and Jew. In the liturgy, of course, two great personalities take center stage. The first is the vision of Isaiah, Chapter 6: 3. Isaiah sees God seated on his throne and he hears the voices of the angels calling Holy, Holy, Holy is the Lord of Hosts, the whole earth is full of His glory. This verse was so powerful in its day, it became part of the Jewish Liturgy. It was part of the 18 recited Benedictions, and the third Benediction of the morning prayer.

It should be noted that there was a liturgical difference between the Palestinian and Babylonian traditions. In Palestine, the Amidah, or Hear of the Morning Prayer, consisted of 18 benedictions. In Babylonia, it consisted of 19 benedictions. In Palestine, the prayer of holiness, called Kedusha, was only recited on Sabbath and festivals days; in Babylonia it was recited every day. The entire service was called the Tefillah. Part of it, the Amediah, was so called because reciting was done standing. It was an ancient Jewish custom to stand during prayer. This custom was based upon Psalm 106:30 *"Then Phineas stood up and spoke judgment"* According to the Talmud, the expression itself means prayer. It was customary to recite four sections in a standing position. The first section was called Avot because it mentioned three patriarchs, who according to tradition recognized God as their Father and as their mentor. The Avot refers to the God of Abraham, Isaac and Jacob who has led his people since their very origin.

The second prayer is called Gevurot, and refers to the power of God's wondrous deeds in providing the needs of every living being. The Gevurot expresses the belief that God's loving kindness extends after death. The highlight of the service begins with a section called Kedushat Hashem. The benediction associated with this section begins with sanctifying God's name It is the Jew's conviction that only God can be sanctified among the children of Israel and only in the midst of a quorum of 10 male adults , this according to Babylonian custom. There were 7 male adults; according to Palestinian ritual.The Kedusha consisted of three scriptural verses. The first was taken from Isaiah Chapter 6 verse 3: *"Holy, Holy, Holy is the Lord of Hosts; the whole earth is full of his glory."* The second was called Barouch, and went like this: ***"Blessed is the presence of the Lord, in His place,"*** taken from Ezekiel 3:12. The third was Yam loch, ***"the Lord will reign forever; the God of Zion until all generations,"*** as taken from Psalm 146:10. Thus, the

Kadusha Section. This section began to be used in all of Jewish Liturgy from the Western Ashkenazic to the Eastern Sephardic, and included even in the perm Persian and Yemenite rituals. All of the meaningful rituals showed the influence of angels upon Jewish ritual.

There were two groups of angels as developed in the Jewish tradition: The Angels of Light and The Angels of Darkness. It is interesting to note that with the discovery of the Dead Sea Scrolls the uncovered war scroll describes the two angels as being of primary importance. The two groups of angels were in perpetual conflict and were believed to fight on the side of two opposing armies in the last battle on the last day when the Angel of Darkness and his army would be destroyed. This is specifically spelled out in the manual of discipline in the Dead Sea Scrolls. *"In the hand of the Prince of Light is a dominion of all the sons of righteousness and in the hand of the Angel of Darkness is the dominion of the sons of evil."* The tradition therefore, had great influence for the Liturgies of both Jews and Christians. In the battle against evil we call upon the angels of Light to assist us when speaking the words of holiness as found in the prayer of the Kedusha. The words proclaim the sanctification of God, both on earth and in heaven, and as in the words of the Prophet Isaiah, the idea of the holiness of God becomes sanctified in the presence of the congregation.

The idea of angels singing hymns of praise to God was so powerful in Jewish tradition that it was incorporated in various different groups of hymns. In these hymns men would join the angels in singing the praise of God. This is what developed in the Kedusha prayers. It also was introduced in the morning service, the Kedusha Yotzer. In this prayer, the description is given of angels singing to God about creation. There were two mystical traditions, one dealing with the spirit of creation and the other dealing with the spirit of the chariot that the Prophet Ezekiel spoke of in chapter 3:12. These mystical ideas became part of the historic Jewish Liturgy and are still part of the spirit of the Liturgy. The Liturgy was influenced by mysticism, which in turn, distinguished the several categories of angels:

Ministering and corrupting angels,
angels of mercy *and*
angels of severe judgment.

Furthermore, angels with masculine characteristics are distinguished from those of feminine qualities. The angels stemming from the highest light came into being on the first day of creation and enjoy eternal life; the others having rebelled against God and subsequently have been consumed by the fire formed on the second day of creation. The angels themselves consist of fire and water according to the account of the four heavenly elements; mercy, strength, beauty, and dominion. The spirit of this mystical tradition of angels came into the Hebrew expression of poetry called Pyetim. The prayers that were incorporated into the prayer book because of the influence of angels played an important part in the service.

We thus find the influence of angels in the recently recovered Dead Sea Scrolls and in a special prayer called the Angelic Liturgy. From this recent discovery we have the following words: *"Before him there is no ceasing. He knows what the world is before it was created, and generation unto generation shall arise those who sleep not and bless thee. They stand before thy glory and bless thy law and extol thee by saying 'Holy, Holy, Holy is the Lord of Hosts, he fills the earth with his glory.' And here my eyes saw all who sleep not, how they stand before him and bless him and say,' Blessed be Thou and blessed be the name of the Lord forever and ever.'"* We see the influence of Ezekiel and Isaiah. Isaiah, with his brief experience of angels in heaven singing to God on his throne, and Ezekiel who sees a vision of a heavenly throne chariot called the Merkada. Here again is evidence of the tremendous influence angels played in Jewish prayers. This tradition also found its way into the early Christian church. We note how angels play an important role in the Gospels and the New Testament as a whole. Early Christians, after all, were Jews who observed the Jewish service and who incorporated it into their revised service in the first century.

The first literal quotation of Isaiah 6:3 is the angelic hymn. It can be found in examples of early Christian literature such as Clement's first Epistles to the Corinthians and Revelations 4:8. We know that Clement was Bishop of Hierapolis in Phrygia during the early part of the second century. He must have known parts of Revelation, such as Chapter 4.

All evidence points to the end of the first century as the time the New Testament was initially put together. As mentioned, the Hymn of the Angels would become part of Christian Liturgy. We also note that we find this hymn in Saint Ignatius and in the writings of the Alexandrian, Clement. This provides us an understanding of how the Jewish tradition of Angels singing came into the Christian tradition. We note in the writing of Clement of Rome: *"Ten thousand times ten thousand waited on him and a thousand more served him and cried Holy, Holy, Holy is the Lord of Hosts and the entire creation is full of thy glory and we, guided by our conscience, and gathered in our place, cried to him that we become sharers in his great and glorious promises."* We note in Revelations 4:8 *"And four beasts had each of them six wings about him; and they were full of eyes within; and they rest not day and night, singing Holy, holy, holy, Lord God Almighty, which was, and is, and is to come."* Clement of Alexandria taught these words; *"Let him teach his son in a way so that we will always praise God just as praising beasts do whom Isaiah spoke of allegorically."* Saint Ignatius says these words. *"This is why, in the symphony of your love, praises of Jesus Christ are sung. But you, the rank and file, should also form a choir so that joining in the symphony of your concord, and by your unity taking a keynote from God, you may with one voice, through Jesus Christ sing a song to the father."*

Finally, as we study the early Christian Liturgy of the first and second centuries, we uncover material the Jews had been singing for over 500 years and now being sung in the early churches. We find it in all parts of the worship service, as the symbolic angelic choir becomes the model for Christian worship. It was so ingrained in the Jewish service, the early Jewish Christians naturally incorporated it into their service. Today, when you hear the words of the Kodosh in the Synagogue, you also find angels in the Sanctus of the Catholic Mass and related parts of the Greek Orthodox Church liturgy.

5)The Scriptural Lesson in the Synagogue and Church

One of the most important parts of Jewish and Christian worship was the reading of the scriptural lesson. While the practice prevails to this day in almost all Oriental religions, it seems probable that the public reading of sacred writings was once a unique feature of the ancient Jewish ritual. It appears to be a distinctive part of ancient Hebrew worship from the beginning. There was as far as we know, no scriptural lesson in the ancient religions of the Philistines or any other of the ancient peoples who lived near Israel. The practice of reading from scripture became the center of Jewish worship It developed gradually in stages, becoming a regular practice about a hundred years before Christianity. It was, without a question, the important development of worship drawing from sources stretching back to ancient Biblical times.

We come face to face with it in the book of Deuteronomy, as we do in the books of Kings, Ezra and Nehemiah. The reading of Torah to the general public was already a practice, introduced by the Prophet Ezra when he brought the people back to their ancient homeland. It was also part and parcel of a tradition believed to have begun in the exile. We have no records to confirm this, but when the people gathered together for worship while they were in exile, they not only read from the Psalms, they also read from the Torah, the five books of Moses, and likely they centered their worship on scriptural readings. We know that certain passages were read on holy days and Sabbaths in the Temple, for we have many sources to confirm that to be the practice. But the synagogue was from the onset, more of an instructional location than a ritual institution. The study of the law and the prophets were more firmly established there than they were in the Temple setting.

In the Temple, the ritual of the sacrificial cult became the important part of main worship and the reading of scripture secondary. In the synagogue, the regular reading of the Torah was practiced in a cycle of choices, later to become the established way of learning the tradition. Each week, selections were read so that one could learn the scripture as well as experience their message. In early Christianity we know that the same practice instituted by the synagogue, was followed by some churches. For some, there was not only a weekly reading, there was also a daily reading of scripture.

Frequently we find in Christian rituals, ancient Jewish traditions that survived all the schisms and strife, dating back to the period when Christianity appeared to be no more than one Jewish sect among others. Thus, if we want to fully understand the relationship between Jewish and Christian worship, we need to study the development of the scriptural lesson in both the earlier mother religion of

Judaism and the later daughter religion of Christianity.

The scriptural lesson was obligatory for the central sanctuary of the Temple. It was obligatory for special occasions, as on the Day of Atonement, when the priest would read the lesson of the day, and on such occasions as the days of Jubilees and the New Moon. Once a year, on the Feast of Tabernacles, the King would visit the Temple, exercise his privilege of reading the day's recessitation, and give an interpretation of his reading. Probably, the sacrifices themselves were accompanied by the recessitation of pertinent laws from the Pentateuch (Torah). It appears the Temple cult contained few regular lessons and no cyclical yearly scriptural readings. Some scholars reject the belief of a scripture lesson as a regular feature of Temple worship in Jerusalem. Whether or not it was a feature, it was not the main part of the Temple ritual.

As far as the synagogue is concerned, the place of scripture readings is of primary importance. There cannot be any doubt that in the ritual of the ancient synagogue, primarily an institution of learning rather than prayer, the regular and continuous lessons from scripture played a central role. Originally the lesson was the substitute for sacrifice, the monopoly feature of the central sanctuary, never to be questioned or abandoned. To the present day, the Jewish ritual has provided for the reading of the scriptural lesson, and those passages assigned to respective Sabbath sacrifices and holy days.

Today, it is customary for three men to stand by the reading of the Torah; the President of the Synagogue (the **parnas**), the reader (the **Baal Kore**), and the man who had been called to read. As the knowledge of the text and its language vanished, over time, the reader recited the entire lesson for the congregation. During the week, three were called to the Torah; on the Sabbath seven were called to the pulpit. Until the 5th and 6th centuries the opportunity to read from scripture belonged first to the priestly families, then to the elders and later to the scholars of merit. The last remnant of this practice is the present custom of calling to the pulpit, first the kohen of a priestly family, then a member of the Levite family, and afterwards the scholar, whether he be a rabbi or layman, or if not available, those approved by the synagogue as dedicated to the reading of the Torah.

In the New Testament, the Gospel of Luke (Lk.4:6), gives us a short description of the scriptural reading in the ancient synagogue. It was recorded that during the days Jesus walked on the earth the president of the synagogue "called him up" and after pronouncing the prescribed eulogies, Jesus read from the Law; then the book of Isaiah was given to Him and he found there the chapter which he subsequently expounded as his homily. Jesus followed the old synagogue tradition of first being called to the reading of the Law and then expounding the scripture he had chosen. Synagogues observe the same scriptural reading practice to this very day.

In most synagogues, whether they be Reform, Conservative, or Orthodox, it is customary for the rabbi or a learned laymen to read from scripture, then give a sermon or a homily on the passage read. In times past in ancient Israel, each man called upon to do his portion would recite the lesson by himself. When Hebrew was replaced by Aramaic or Greek, an interpreter was appointed to translate the original text, sentence for sentence, into the vernacular of the language of the time. The practice of translating was not only limited to the synagogue, we learn from the early church in Jerusalem that it was a practice to have someone read the text either in Greek or Latin and then translate it into the vernacular of the time. We find the reader employed both in the synagogue and in the church to be schooled in being able to read and chant the scripture of the

53

time. Later, it became the duty of the priesthood that a select number studying for the priesthood read and serve as presenters or cantors. Often the presenters had to substitute for the regular reader. In later centuries the presenters became the appointed cantors and ministers of the congregation.

The early church, in following the traditions of the synagogue, instituted the reading of scripture as an accepted custom and tradition, followed by a translation and a sermon illustrating the meaning of the reading. When did the lessons actually begin to be read as a regular part of the synagogue service? Most scholars believe that by the time of Ezra, the lessons were read on special occasions and probably every Saturday in the synagogue. Later, in Jerusalem when many houses of worship were erected near the main Temple, portions of the Pentateuch or Torah, were read in these regular Sabbath assemblies and on Mondays and Thursdays, the typical market days for the people who lived in rural areas not near the Temple. That custom has survived to this very day. A portion of these weekly regular lessons were read on holy days, fast days, and days of special significance, as special lessons.

Two types of lessons came from the reading of scripture: The regular reading of the lesson of the week, comprising the entire Torah "Pentateuch". Today it is arranged in annual cycles, beginning with the Sabbath after Tabernacles and ending on the last day of Tabernacles, the festival of "Rejoicing over the law." Secondly, another short lesson was assigned on every Sabbath or holy day, called the Haphtarah (or dismissal, because it was used at the end of the service). This lesson was selected from the Prophetic books. Consequently, there were two distinct lessons, one from the Torah and one from the Prophets. From each source a specific lesson was taken for weekly study. The Prophetic lessons were broken up by chapters to be selected for study that week. The rabbis selected portions from the Prophetic readings that had a connection with the Torah readings. Wherever a specific subject was read in the Pentateuch, the rabbis found a parallel passage to be read from the Prophets. Hence, the Prophetic lessons consisted of whole chapters that became a part of the scriptural lesson of the week. The selection of weekly lessons follow closely what churches today do more frequently than in the past. We note that in the course of the parallel relationship between church and synagogue, selections of scripture readings depend upon the season of the year, and whatever the season of year calls for will be the readings that are assigned for that specific day. The church has also made an assignment of readings from scriptures as part of their ritual and prayer service. It has become a tradition to read lessons from scripture for special seasons of the year, applied to the special holiday of the time.

How were the readings of the Torah performed in the synagogue? The scroll was solemnly taken from the ark. Verses were sung from the Psalms and displayed to the assembled congregation. The reader then chanted the special section of the day in a manner determined by rigid tradition, a tradition that became part of a system of scripture readings each week. Every week there were assigned readings with no changes.The reading was done in cantilation, called by the Greek name Trop. Trop represented a form of chanting that has been carried on to the present time.

There were special signs for the reading of the Torah in Hebrew. A threefold purpose defines these signs.

First, to provide the scriptural text an elaborate punctuation that would preclude any none Hebrew reference to the meaning of the words and phrases.

Secondly,the canilation or the chanting was brought

55

into a determined mode so that whoever read, did so from a tradition that followed what was done in all synagogues.

Thirdly, the accentuation marks followed the rules of Hebrew grammar known at the time, and as sent by the tradition of the forefathers.

The reading from scripture in chant form became part of the musical liturgy of the early church. The early church followed a tradition of chanting scripture in a way that followed a distinct mood, and handed down from one priesthood to the next.

The closely related development of lessons in the synagogue followed a long process, evidencing changes prior to becoming formalized in its present form. The Torah lesson itself was arranged a century or so before the birth of Christianity, while the Prophetic readings required another three or four centuries before they finally would be put into codification. We know that these readings were becoming well established at the time Jesus came on the scene. The reading of the week itself, called Sedra, was likely repeated in most, if not all, synagogues during Jesus' time on earth.

There were opinionated differences as to the readings in the Synagogues in Jerusalem and the readings in the synagogues outside of the center of Jerusalem, or in the rural sections. We are not completely clear about the exact differences between the two, but it is clear from historic evidence that differences did exist between the various readings from one community to the other.

The passage in Luke 4:16 reveals some interesting aspects about the customs practiced by rural communities in ancient Israel. We know, for instance through sound scholarship, that the understanding of the word *"he found"* indicates that the Prophetic portion had previously been prepared and marked in the scrolls by an official, and that Jesus could therefore easily find the prescribed passage.

Since lengthy unfoldings and searching in scrolls were not permitted on the Sabbath, we can conclude that the Prophetic cycle was already established or just beginning to come into practice.

In ancient times, the full cycle of Jerusalem lessons ran for three years, while in Babylonia it ran for one year. After the sixth or seventh century, Palestine and the entire Diaspora accepted the annual Babylonia. The short cycle began after Tabernacles and continued on for fifty Sabbaths. Four special Sabbaths had lessons of their own handed down from former times. The portion for the festivals, the holy days, new moons, and fast days did not form part of the regular readings, because they were entirely different. The three-year cycle probably started on the first or second Sabbath of the Hebrew month of Nisan, depending on the date of the Passover, and ended on the first Sabbath of Adar, the twelfth month. In a leap year it was the thirteenth month. Inserted between the end of the triennial cycle and its commencement were four special Sabbaths, whose portions were read annually. The same practice pertained to all festivals and holy days that interrupted regular reading cycles. These facts lead us to believe that the Jerusalem synagogue set a standard for all synagogues throughout the world. So, no matter what country or what place you would be in, you would still be doing the same reading of the week. That created a unity among all synagogues and developed a program that teachers would be able to prepare readings of the week in anticipation of the Sabbath service. We know that the practice of reading scripture in the early church became a regular part of the church service from our studies of the writings of Paul, Justin, and Clement. Later, the early church would begin to read from the Gospels as well as the Hebrew texts. This practice began around the second half of the third century as the church developed its own special scripture readings for each week. It became part of church tradition to not only read the scriptures, but chant them as well, as had been done in the synagogue. It was clear that the Christian homily was based on the scriptural reading of the week, another carryover from Synagogue practice. We know the early church developed a regular system of readings that included specific readings for the week day services. The Eastern churches have preserved more of this type of continuous lesson reading to the present day. It was the historic task of Christian and Jewish scholars to create a framework which followed a specific system of readings for each Holy day of the year. In Catholic Churches, with their overlapping cycles of ecclesiastical priorities, this proved to be an effective way of following the system the synagogue had earlier established for remembering Hebrew events for each week of the lunar year.

The Byzantine church follows the old Jewish principle of naming the Sunday after the scriptural lesson of the day. In the Roman rite, the situation appears to be different. We find no trace of the Greek and Syrian Orthodox system in the Roman rite. As was done in the synagogue, the Psalms are chanted before and between lessons. As in the synagogue, the Gospels and the Old Testament lessons are chanted according to a special tradition that in many ways have followed the cantilation that was used in the synagogue.

The church of earliest Christianity, the Armenian church, was the first expression of the state church Christianity would took in the fourth century. We have an educated impression that the early Armenian church followed closely the Jerusalem rite at the time. In the early Armenian church the same verses of scripture were read that were read by the Jews. The Armenian system of readings flowed into the entire early church, with the obvious exceptions of the Easter period when readings were strictly taken from the New Testament. It is an impressive fact of history that the Armenian Church closely followed both the readings from the Pentateuch, as well as the readings from the Prophets. That tradition is carried on to today. We can now see that both the early church and the early synagogue carried on a tradition of mutual scriptural readings that became an important part in the liturgical life of the worship service.

There is a demonstrative bond that exists between Church and Synagogue to the present day. Whether you visit a synagogue or a church, you are bound to hear a scriptural reading that has its ancient source in the time of Ezra, when the people returning from exile found new hope and inspiration in their weekly scriptural lessons.

CHAPTER THREE
Synagogue and early Church understandings of worship

1)   **Liturgical responses of early Church and Synagogue**

Liturgy is the foundation of organized worship. As such, it is not something that simply belongs to the priesthood, but belongs to the entire congregation. We know that the community of both synagogue and church wanted to share in worship and did share in the liturgical ritual by singing the word. There were multiple factors associated with the development of Judaism, Islam and Christianity, that demanded the participation of the entire community. An abundance of material in pagan cults tells the same story. We know, for instance, that in the historic development of the liturgy, for both synagogue and church, the congregation felt a need to participate in various responses as developed in both faith communities. One of those interesting features associated with the development of liturgies is how unique traditional features shape liturgical responses. The earliest response, we know of, is the ritual meaning of "amen," known to be an affirmation, an oath, and even signifying acceptance of the prior statement. It is, in some respects, the most important acclamation arising in worship. As an oath, the "amen" was specifically prescribed in the legalistic passage of Deuteronomy 27:15. It also serves as a usual affirmation after eulogies or praises, as prescribed by Rabbinic teachers. In the Bible, it appears chiefly as an expression of acceptance, such as in First Chronicles 16:36, Psalm 72:19-106, and Psalm 4:8. Typically, the "amen" came at the very end of the service. In Judaism, the "amen" was considered necessary for the close of certain prayers. We know from the report of the Jewish services in Alexandria, that the congregation was required and requested to respond to the "amen" by a signal of a white flag. In the synagogue of today, the Cantor must not continue with a blessing, or **beraka**, until congregation has responded with the" amen."

The "amen" parts were taken over by the church. Having followed the example of the Apostles, themselves Jewish, and thus familiar with the rules of Jewish worship, the matter of "amen" entering Christian worship was a matter of course. We find it, for example, in First Corinthians 14:16, and Romans 9:5. The "amen" holds a special significance in the Apocalyptic literature, as seen in Revelation 5:14, 19:14. Here, as was common in synagogue worship, it took the form that would become an intragal part of the life of the church. It carried on a heritage, the early church did not want to break with. In the Book of Revelation we find, *"Grace be unto you and peace - from Jesus Christ to him be glory and dominion forever and ever, amen"*. In the Judaeo / Christian tradition, the word "amen" is even personalized. *"These things sayeth the amen, the faithful and true virtues, the beginning of the creation of God"*. This conception is in accordance with the Judaic tradition that believed the congregation had a moral responsibility to respond with the "amen." In church liturgical use, the "amen" is typically understood as a strong affirmation of the prayer just spoken.

Concerning its musical rendition, there are slight differences between the synagogue and the church. We know that Christianity established early trained choirs, consisting of monks or men from the lower clergy, who tended to stretch their musical performance of the "amen." Sometimes the long "amen" actually became part of an ongoing tradition. We find evidence of that in all early Christian liturgies

.

In Judaism, trained choirs were generally not available and never available before the ninth century of the common era. Therefore, the "amen" remained what it originally was, a simple congregational response. In the early church it became popular to extend the "amen" and repeat it as a way of making a full and spiritual response to prayer.

Another refrain that became popular was the "hallelujah," found in the Book of Psalms. The "hallelujah" became part of the newly designed liturgical Mass. In fact, soon after the inception of the Mass the "hallelujah" became the most popular response of church services. The church originally borrowed it from the synagogue, then developed it to an elaborate degree. Even today, at special times of the church year, it is one of the most popular responses in worship.

A response called "hosanna," held an important part in both Jewish and Christian liturgy. In Judaism it originally symbolized a two fold significance; first, that of an appeal to the King of Kings, God, and secondly, that of a cry for salvation. Both meanings are demonstrated in the Hebrew text of the Tanakh. In the Christian tradition, the original meaning, as found in Matthew 21:9 and in Mark 11:9-10, connoted the same things; an appeal of homage to the royalty of God and a plea for salvation. This second meaning is observed by a literal translation of the Hebrew, but was lost in the Christian development of the Mass. Rather than becoming an appeal to royalty, it became an appeal to the belief that the Messiah has already been here and will return again.

In Judaism, the royal Messianic notion of the "hosanna" was mostly discarded as soon as it became the watchword of the new faith of Christianity. The early synagogue did not want to associate itself with this tradition and dropped it completely from the regular Jewish service. What the synagogue dropped, the church renewed and the "hosanna" has now become an intricate part of regular Christian service in every denomination, and is closely associated with the center of Christian worship. On Palm Sunday, and a time after Easter, the musical role of "hallelujah" was intoned and the cry of the "hosanna" that accompanied Jesus' entrance into Jerusalem was repeated.

In the synagogue, the "hosanna" was a verse in the Hillel prayers, coming from Psalm 118 and chanted during all festivals. But only during the season of Tabernacles, the **Succoth** harvest festival when the **Hosanot** was chanted as a kind of processional, did the "hosanna" stand out as a distinctive refrain in the service. It was and still is rendered responsively according to the old Talmudic interpretation and rule.

Another favorite response in the service was the word "selah," whose meaning is still somewhat obscure. The Greek translation of the Tanakh, or Septuagint, translated it as referring to an instrumental interlude. It occurs almost exclusively in the Psalms and has been taken over by Christianity without any change. Frankly, it stands for an "amen" or similar affirmation. Many have suggested that it was a tradition of the old Temple and used to conclude a section of the service. It is sung / recited at the end of a passage and understood to mean, "So shall it be". No further Jewish attention was paid to this affirmation once it became part of an ongoing Christian tradition.

What is interesting in the development of the Christian liturgy is the fact that the kyrie eleison, which means deliver us or "Lord have mercy on us", became a central part of the Christian service. What is interesting about the kyrie is that it was not mentioned in the Apostolic Fathers or any of the early church fathers before Saint John Chrysostom. It simply began being used in

Antioch and from there traveled to Jerusalem and then throughout the Christian world. It has been presented as the formal opening of the Mass at Roman Catholic Churches. It has, in fact, become a very powerful part of the Roman Mass as well as a significant part of the Eastern Rite.

There was another response called "maranatha," meaning, "Lord come ye." We find this response in the writings of the early church, particularly in the letters of Paul and the Didache. It has never become a significant part of the Christian service, and nothing is known about its original musical rendering.

Of all the responses, only the "amen," the "hallelujah" and the "kyrie" have come to have important liturgical significance for both Judaism and Christianity.The fact that "selah" did not attain the same importance lies with the various changes that took place in the liturgy. The "selah" and the "maranatha," were no longer understood by the congregation and thus fell into disuse.

Judaism has maintained certain words as key traditional concepts. Jewish and Christian liturgies have both linked their traditions with these words to reflect a common bond of religious tradition and consciousness and hopefully elements of a harmonious tradition.

2) **Cleansing and lighting the Menorah**

The Midrash tells us that when the tabernacle was completed, Moses and the children of Israel rejoiced, but Aaron, the high priest was unhappy. Why was that? When Aaron saw the lavish gifts, which the chieftains had contributed to the Tabernacle, his heart was sad, because he himself had no precious gift to offer. Thereupon, God reassured him: "*Your part is more glorious then theirs, for you will light the Menorah*".

When Aaron learned that his task was also to clean the lamps before he kindled the light, he was aggravated and said: *"You don't need a priest to clean the lamps; anyone can do that. Is that such a privilege?"* Then the angel explained to Aaron: *"When a man is sick, the physician tries to find the cause of the ailment and to remove it. It is easy to light the Menorah. Anyone can do that, but it takes a special person to clean the lamps and remove whatever would dim the brightness of the flame. You are like the skillful physician, because you will make it possible for the light to burn brightly."* Aaron was then satisfied in his heart and fulfilled his mission.

There are two phases to our religious life. They are to walk together on Shabbat as a people, and to kindle the spark of individual faith by kindling the candles for Shabbat. By doing so, we cleanse the heart so that the spark of faith itself becomes a bright flame.

For Jews, the State of Israel is a place where we have rekindled the lamps and have undertaken the task to rebuild that land so that the light of this faith will shine upon the world. In spite of troubling times, the light of peace is now beginning to shine and we must learn, not only to rekindle that light, but more importantly, to cleanse the light and the lamps. For all of us, the cleansing of the heart is a primary challenge that the spark of faith may become a bright flame that all may see.

These are difficult times when relatively few of us are really fulfilling the command to rekindle the spark of faith. We will need faith in the difficult days of the peace process. The more we cleanse our hearts, the more we cleanse our faith with a hope that peace can be established in the land of father Abraham. That faith must never be extinguished. We need to rekindle it daily, cleansing our hearts and minds of worry, suspicion and doubt that the triumph of peace and its flame of hope may radiate to all parts of our world, that from Zion will go forth, not only the law, but a new light and a new faith.

3) **Doxology in the Synagogue and early Church**

The doxology expresses another common element between Jewish and Christian worship. You may ask the question, "What is a doxology?" The clear and general definition is that it is a means to declare and proclaim glory. This was the way in which it was used in both Jewish and Christian worship. The doxology became part of a common liturgical tradition. The use of "Dora" meant a sense of praise and glory given to God. We find this in typical Jewish worship. We also locate the Dora in a passage from the tiny letter to Timothy, 6:16 *"The Lord of Lords, who has immortality, dwelling in light unapproachable; who no man has seen, nor can see; to whom be honor and power eternal. Amen"*

The word doxology comes from the Greek. It was not merely a benediction, but praise unto infinity. The term Doxolodia became part of an older tradition that grew up in both synagogue and church. It was found in the prayers and response of both services from their beginnings.

Originally, prayers were spontaneous and flexible; later they would be fixed and final. In the early church the doxology was employed as a hedge against harassers and disbelievers. The early church, experiencing the pressure of Arianism, and other agnostic sects, formed two doxological prayers, as presented in the apostolic constitutions. One was a poetic Paraphrase of Luke 2:14, commonly known as the Gloria in Excelisis. Soon this doxology would become an integral part of the Catholic Mass. It was spoken in these terms: *"Glory be to the father, to the Son and to the Holy Spirit now and always forever."* The emphasis lies obviously on two elements: one "The Trinity" and two "Its preexistence from the beginning of time." This became part of a tradition, still sung and spoken to this day in the Mass.

67

One of the interesting factors is that this doxology originally could be found in the Psalms, for example: Psalm 106:48 *"And blessed be His glorious name forever and let the whole earth be filled with his glory, amen".* Also: *"Blessed be the Lord, the God of Israel from everlasting to everlasting, amen".* If we compare the Christian doxology with the Jewish doxology, we find that there is a common source from which both spring. That is the Ketubim. (Wisdom Writings in English).

In the liturgy of the ancient Temple there was, as was noted, certain prayers that carried over from synagogue to church. This was especially true in relation to the refrains, which the congregation recited. It was part of a tradition in which the Jew would begin a blessing by the words, barouch atoh (Blessed art thou). This then became part of the Christian benediction. Though they, the synagogue and the church, differed in theology they used almost the same vocal forms.

In the study of the liturgy of Rabbinic Judaism, we frequently encounter certain doxologies that became an important part of Jewish services. They were;

1) *"Praise be His name, who glorious kingdom is forever and ever; "*
2) *"Praise be the Lord, to whom all praise is due forever and ever;"*
3) *"Holy, Holy, Holy is the Lord of Host, the whole earth is full of his glory;"* and
4) *"Praise be his glorious name unto all eternity."*

These formula doxologies have a number of elements in common:

1) They are all genuine responses
2) They all contain the idea of God's infinity in time.
3) They are frequently mentioned together as one family of prayers and sometimes even considered together.

4) They have replaced the old Temple doxology, taken
        from the end of the five books of the Psalms

One of the interesting factors in the study of the liturgy of both the Mass and the synagogue contains the simple the fact that these doxologies became firmly implanted in the structure of both services.

Giving praise to God's kingdom was used in the Temple as a response for every blessing ever made. When the Temple was destroyed, the synagogue continued the tradition by pronouncing the Shema *"Here Oh Israel, the Lord is one"* and then quietly reciting the prayer *"Praise be His name whose glorious kingdom is forever and ever,"* each holy day. It has become the center of Jewish worship and the very end of the service commemorating the most holiest day of the year, the Day of Atonement.

There has always been a difference in theology between the two faiths but as you study the prayers of the early church, you may note how influenced they were by the special prayer called, the Kedusha. In the liturgy of the synagogue, the Kedusha appears in three main types:
1. Of the early morning service;
2. The Kedusha, the intricate part of the Amidah 18 prayers, recited in the morning;
3. The Kedusha, as the end of a weekdays morning service.

What was the Kedusha? The Kedusha took the words of Isaiah 6:3 *"Holy, Holy, Holy is the Lord of Host, the whole earth is full of his glory."* It was a doxology, one that became the center of Jewish worship and possibly one of the oldest known traditions, that have come to us from the Temple.

When we study the prayers of the early church, we hear this doxology as praise and thanksgiving. That is how the early church fathers heard it as evidenced from their writings. Clement teaches his people by speaking the words, *"Grant us hope in thy name, the first source of all creation; open the eyes of our hearts to know thee that thou alone art the highest and remains holy among the holy ones".* This prayer parallels the third prayer of the eighteenth benediction that speaks the words, *"Thou art holy, thy name is holy, and thy worshipers proclaim thy holiness. Blessed art thou oh God, the holy God."*

The early church used invitational formulas chiefly before the Mass of the faithful. All of them are part of an ancient tradition, dating back to the first and second Temple, where the high priest would call the people to worship; after which they responded by reciting the words: *"Praise be his name forever and ever."*

Notice that in the liturgy of Clement of Rome, it begins with the call to worship: *"Turn ye to God, bow your heads and pray."* We find in the Syriac liturgy. *"Come ye, let us praise the Lord and sing about our salvation."* It follows in the liturgy of Constantinople *"Praise be thou, oh God, always now and forever and always, amen."* We find the same sort of wording in the apostolic constitutions in which the words are recited: *"Ye children, praise the Lord, sing praise to the name of the Lord."*

The importance of the form and rendering of the boruch (Blessed) and its response, is greatly enhanced by the fact that it serves to call the people together for public worship, and with that in mind, spells out the reason for worship itself. The call motivates the congregation to a spirit of highest activity, that of bringing God into our midst.

In the early church, church fathers such as Origin, stated that each proper prayer should end in a doxology, or praise to God. Actually, we find doxologies throughout the New Testament. One fact must be stressed, for it is often neglected or not completely understood. I am referring to the fact that in the Gospels we encounter only one doxology and that at the end of the Lord's Prayer. The authenticity of this single passage moreover, is considered doubtful and has been disputed amongst Christian scholars. The usual explanation for the Gospels not including liturgies is that the Gospel writers were dealing with the history and background of the life of Jesus and his teachings. Individual prayers were not thought to be a part of that tradition, except in the Lord's Prayer. It should be remembered that early Christianity was also a movement of the poor and meek; its roots lying in the rural sections of Galilee. Jerusalem, the priests and many of the rabbis, were opposed to men from the country, despising them for their relative ignorance of ritual and practice.

The small local synagogue with its simple and direct way of praying to God was the real birthplace of Christian liturgy. There was no room in these communal houses of worship for rigid and solemn formulas, such as you find in the Temple doxologies of the high priestly cult of Jerusalem. This would explain the almost complete absence of all liturgical materials in the Gospels. The literature of Paul however, is filled with many doxologies, being part of Paul's life and training. In his case, the doxologies were direct translations of familiar Hebrew prayers. The reference to Christ that Paul and others from the scribal background make, may be because Christ is considered the high priest of the new community. As we read in the early church father, Polycarp: *"Thee I praise, Thee I glorify, thou everlasting and heavenly high priest, Jesus Christ, through whom we are to be glory, to thee and to him and to the Holy Spirit."*

The direct addressing of the Lord classifies this piece as part of the doxology, which became by this time, a routine part of Christian tradition. We note the strong relationship that these prayers, both in Jewish and Christian traditions, exhibited as part of a liturgy that was so similar in structure and words. Though the church and the synagogue differed in theology, liturgy bound them together, as they praised the same God in almost the same words, the one spoken and sung in Hebrew and the other spoken and sung in Latin or Greek.

4) **Messianic Blessings in Jewish and Christian Traditions**

To understand the background of the Messianic Blessing in the Jewish tradition, it is necessary to understand how these messianic ideas came to be. What were their roots? How did they enter into the Christian tradition as it relates to Jesus and the early church. We understand, as we look at the literature of the Dead Sea Scrolls, about Jewish Messianic expectations. Rabbinic literature provides us with the most significant sources of piecing together the puzzle of the various and diversified Jewish traditions concerning the appearance of the Messiah and their influences on the beginnings of Christianity.

Until recently, Christian scholars had not been aware of the Jewish roots of the Messiah. With the availability of Rabbinic literature for all to view and understand, we now can recognize that there was a definite connection between Jewish Messianic ideas and the Christian Messianic ideas. In a number of ways they are intertwined in one historic development of ideas.

When we study the Messianic Blessing we note that both in the Gospels and in Midrash, Pesikta, Derava, and Kahana clues appear as to how how the whole idea of a Messianic Blessing came to be. As we pursue and analyze these ideas in the literature of the Midrash, we uncover the Rabbinic origin of Messiah, contemporary with the development of First and Second Century Christian literature.

The Messianic Blessing appears as a climax to a sermon located in the Midrash; a collections of sermons the rabbi's gave. It is here we find this concept: *"I will greatly rejoice in the Lord, my soul shall rejoice in God; for he has clothed me with garments of salvation. He has covered me with the robes of righteousness"* (Isaiah 61:10). This concept becomes the primary text for the entire sermon. It concludes with a blessing, in many ways parallel to another Midrash called Pesikta Rabbati, as well as in another collection of Midrash called Yalkut Hamakiri. We will present three parallel texts to show the difference in the preservation of a Messianic song as it appeared in the three different sermons.

In the first Midrash of Pesikta Derava Kahana we discover these words: *"The splendor of the garment he puts on Messiah will stream forth from the world's end to the world's end, as implied in the words, 'As a bridegroom puts on a priestly diadem Israel will make use of his light and say, Blessed is the hour in which the Messiah was created."*

When we pursue it even further, we note almost the same words used by the same three texts. All of them use the words *"Blessed is the womb from whence he came! Blessed is the generation whose eyes behold him! Blessed is the eye, which has been given the privilege of seeing him. Whose lips open with the blessing and peace, whose diction is pure delight, whose garments are glory and majesty, who is confident and serene in his speech, the utterance of whose tongue is pardoned with forgiveness, whose prayer is sweet savor, whose supplication during study is purity and holiness."* They respond. *"Blessed are Israel, how much is laid up for them! As it is said 'Oh how abundant is the goodness which thou has laid up for them that revere thee.'"* When we study these same words, almost identically worded in the three different orders of Midrashim, we know that this must have had an important role in the development of the concept of the Messianic Blessing that was prophesied to fall on Israel.

The difference between the three versions of the Messianic Blessing as they appear in Pesikta Rabbati, Yalkut Hamakiri, and Pesikita Derava Kahana are minor. Yet it seems inevitable that this was an important part of the Messianic hope and Blessing which the Jews were awaiting after so long a period of suffering and persecution. The triumph of the coming Messiah was believed to be the vehicle to deliver them out of that suffering and persecution and bring about the kingdom of God's glory upon this earth.

It is interesting to note that the Dead Sea Scrolls example well know beliefs concerning the coming of the Messiah from the line of Aaron and from the seed of David. We know that the community of the renewed covenant that lived by the Dead Sea were the creators of the Scrolls. This community eagerly awaited the Messiah to appear in triumph and institute a new order. They made great sacrifices to live in the vast, lonely and uninhabited desert by the Dead Sea. We know they hoped and believed in the coming of a Messiah and we also know that they had two different kinds of Messiahs. There was the priestly Messiah and the Davidic Messiah. We note, as we study the Scrolls about what these people truly believed, what they saw in their future. They looked forward to a Davidic Messiah who would come of the royal household of David. His reign would be confined to political leadership for the future. However, at the same time they also believed in a high priest Messiah, who would be focused on a cultic leadership as one who would lead the people through the religious and ritual traditions of the past.

The priestly Messiah was to perform the atonement rites and all the duties that the high priest once performed in the ancient Temple. This gives us a clue as to the blessing that each Messiah would bring to the people. It was something the people looked forward to with great anticipation. Living in a time of great uncertainty, their hope was that the coming of a Messiah of Aaron and of Israel would fulfill their hopes and their dreams.

The teacher of righteousness was considered an historic living temporal prophet, while unknown to us now, then visibly experienced by members of this community. From the scroll writings it appears that he was considered an exiled high priest, the true interpreter of the law whom God had sent to them in difficult times. After the assumed death of the teacher of righteousness, members were asked to follow his teaching and his interpretation of the law until the coming of another prophet and then the anticipated priestly Messiah. The prophet was to be like Moses, someone God would raise up to tell all his brethren what God had commanded him to say, but the teaching of the law was to be from the priestly Messiah who, like Aaron, would officiate at the great altar of God in the new spiritual Temple. He would bring about the fulfillment of the kingdom of God.

In the Prophecy of Malchi we note that the coming of the Messiah would be announced by the forerunner of Elijah. The forerunner will prepare the final judgment and restore the basic foundation for the kingly Messiah who, in turn, will fulfill the hope and expectation of a messianic age.

We note that this teaching of the Dead Sea Community gives us an understanding of passages in the New Testament that envisioned Elijah as the forerunner of the Messiah, and a possible identification between the Dead Sea Community and the writers of the New Testament. The belief in the New Testament that Elijah must come first before the Messiah or the Son of Man, is recorded in Mark 9:2-13 and Matthew 17:1-13. The ideal of Messiahship is, according to the scribes, a declaration of the messianic sonship of Jesus as one who suffers, dies and rises again.

This popular belief lies in the background to the question certain Jews had of joining Jesus. Was he the true

Messiah? Has Elijah the Prophet, announced and prepared the way of his recognition as the true Messiah. In many passages in the Gospels, from narratives of the annunciation until the passion narratives, we find the formulation of the idea of the Son of God, the Son of the Most High, the Messiah, the Son of Man, and The King of the Jews. These titles show that Jesus was regarded as the King Messiah on the one hand. On the other hand, he is regarded as the priestly character who appears in the Gospels when he institutes the Lord's Supper, giving himself over as a perfect victim for many, for the forgiveness of sins, and to seal the new covenant. Jesus takes on himself the task of universal redemption that Isaiah had assigned in his Sermon to the Lord. What appears in Luke 4:16-21 also reveals the interrelationship between the Messianic idea as offered in the Gospels and that offered in the Dead Sea Community.

During the period of the second Temple, there was a belief that the coming of the Messiah would bring a blessing to the whole world. W may note that this now appears in Rabbinic literature, especially in the Midrash where we have words in the messianic song in Pesikta Derava Kahana specifically speaking of the Messianic Blessing: *"Blessed is the house in which the Messiah was created. Blessed is the womb from whence he came. Blessed is the generation whose eyes beheld him. Blessed is the eye, which has been given privilege of seeing him."*

We can't help but notice that in the Gospel of Luke we have words very similar to that which are in Rabbinic literature. In Luke, we have the words of this type blessing. *"Blessed are you among women and blessed is the fruit of your womb... Blessed is she who believed the generations will call me blessed... Blessed are the eyes who see you when you see.. For I tell you that many prophets and kings desire to see what you see, and did not see it, and to hear what hear and did not hear it."*

These three texts taken from Luke give us an understanding of the parallels we find in Rabbinic literature. We can well understand that the concept of the Messianic Blessings found in the Gospel of Luke, are based upon the Midrash we have just described.

The New Testament contains numerous remnants of early Messiah ideas that have their roots in Jewish sources. Before one can fully understand the Christology that evolved within Christianity, it is desirable to investigate the Jewish world that provided the background and traditions for these teachings. Jesus appears to display a high awareness of his own Messianic role, according to the available texts, paralleled but not identical with the various concepts of the Jewish Messiah. The great difference between the Messiah in Jewish tradition, with that of the Messiah in Christian tradition is the predicted national liberation the former offers. In the New Testament the Messiah represents more of a universal ideal, one that would become a part of Christian theology.

5) **The meaning of Liturgy for Synagogue and early Church**

The bond between the synagogue and the church was not only to be found in their practice of charity, but also in worship and especially in the prayers of service. Knowledge of Jewish worship in Judea at the time of Jesus and the Apostles is indispensable if we would trace the roots of the later and more fully developed liturgies of Judaism and Christianity.

The whole idea of Liturgy would have meant little to Jesus and his disciples, as well as to the rabbis of the synagogue. For the term Liturgy is a Greek term and we find it's use in Plato. In Aristotle the term was expanded to mean anyone who rendered a service of any kind. Even a juggler could qualify.

With the spread of the Greek translation of the Hebrew Bible, the Septuagint, the term "Liturgy" narrowed to fit the strict religious activity. The Hebrew words Eved, Avoda (servant, service), kohen (priest) tziva mitzvah (constitute, command, appoint, privilege), were usually translated by the Greek words Liturgy and it's derivations. As we find in the English language today, the association of servant, service, and office official, are often used interchangeably, so Hebrew has preserved these ancient ideas using different words. Gradually, the term "Liturgy" would become known by both Jews and Christians as referring almost exclusively to worship.

No one has understood the meaning of "Liturgy" better than the Apostle Paul, the Pharisee of the Pharisees, who knew all the Hebrew equivalences, associated with the Greek word "Liturgy." In his epistles, he mentions various activities, such as civil office, charity, missionary work, and personal services of a friend, all differentiated by three or four Hebrew words, as "Liturgia." At a later time, these various meanings faded away, until only the meaning of an order of public worship remained, specifically referring to the Eucharistic service.

There is no question that Jesus was acquainted with the practices of both the Temple and the Synagogue. The Temple and the Synagogue were the main institutions, around which the spiritual life of the Jewish people existed. The Temple especially played a major role in the life of the people, for they were commanded to be there three times during the calendar year.

What was the service "liturgy" in the second Temple? It had originally been initiated by Ezra and Nehemiah. That "Liturgy," in part, utilized psalms sung by the Levites. Ben Sira describes the cultic practice of his time this way: *"After the sacrifices were offered, the Levites started with their songs. While the whole people assembled. The High Priest would bless the people who had prostrated themselves."*

Ben Sira also gives a list of benedictions, several of which have remained standard elements in the "Liturgy" of today. The amidah (prayers recited while standing) are very much the same as they were given in the Temple. Example the opening verses in vensura where it says: *"Give thanks to the Lord, to our Redeemer, who gathers the outcasts of Israel."* In the amidah we read: *"Blessed art thou Oh Lord, who has gathered the outcasts of thy people Israel."* We know from the reading of Ben Sira and also from the Mishnah that the priests would recite the Decalogue (Ten Commandments) each morning, the paragraph of the Shema (Hear Oh Israel) and parts of what we now call the Amediah or priestly benediction.

The Temple played the major role in the religious life of the people. There were always those who resented the Temple, as there were priests who resented the Synagogue. This contention would later play out in the formulation of political parties. The priestly party became the Sadducees and members of the synagogues were primarily represented by the Pharisees.

During the second Temple, another sanctuary would develop in Israel - the sanctuary that was destined to replace the Temple after its destruction in 70 CE. This sanctuary was unique in its purpose, for it was dedicated to the study of Holy Scripture and prayer without sacrificial rites. Its origin seems to date back to the exilic era, when people would congregate for worship and divine instruction. Some scholars believe Ezekiel was instrumental in organizing this type of sanctuary while the Israelites were held in Babylon. Upon their return to Jerusalem, Ezra instituted public instruction on the Sabbath and during festivals, that required a house of assembly called "Beit

Hakensseth," later to be known by its Greek name as "the Synagogue." The Synagogue was primarily a lay institution, while the Temple held a monopoly on priests. In keeping with the plan Ezra proposed, the country was divided into 24 sections. Each section would send representatives to Jerusalem twice a year for a period of one week. The duty of these representatives was to attend daily sacrifices. They would fast 4 days of the week from Monday through Thursday and make their prayers on the weekend. At home, the people of a geographic section would congregate in their synagogues and read the first chapter of Genesis, divide it into six portions and perform the same devotional exercises as the representatives in Jerusalem. Here, we have the nucleus for regular daily services for two weeks each year. In time the practice was extended to last the whole year.

The reason for this institution was a popular demand of the people to share in the cult. With the increase in knowledge of the prophetic teachings, as spelled out in scripture, it became clear to the people that not only the priests but every human being should have access to God. The high and the simple may approach God without an intermediator. The great voices from amongst the people taught them that it is even their duty to pray daily. From these sources fixed patterns of benedictions and prayers appeared, initially dating as far back as Ezra's assembly.

The institution of "the House of Assembly" spread throughout the Jewish world. By the end of the 1st century CE there existed no less than 394 synagogues in Jerusalem. This would lead us to believe the synagogue began to take on an important role in the life of the people. It would later become the heir to the central Temple and the primary vehicle Judaism would erect to survive to the present time long after the Romans destroyed of the great Temple.

From various sources we learn that during the era of

the second Temple, the Synagogue's main service was centered on the Shema, as well as the first three and last three benedictions, and other prayers addressing forgiveness of sin, thanksgiving, and petition requests. Following the exile, the tradition of the synagogue included the practice of reading from the scriptures on Sabbath, and during festivals. Mondays through Thursdays became the chief periods of study time. Likewise, there followed readings of the Book of Esther during Purim, and the chanting of Hallel (psalms 113-118) during Passover eve. For several other occasions, the psalms became a central part of the service. Other benedictions were used as grace after meals with yet additional prayers introduced.

The normal custom of the synagogue was to pray three times daily: once in the morning, once in the afternoon, and once in the evening. The three times practice was based on Daniel 6:11 *"And he kneeled upon his knees three times a day and prayed and gave thanks before God"*. And also in Psalms 55:18 *"At evening, morning, and at noon, will I pray, and cry aloud: and he shall hear my voice"*. These instituted practices were considered legal and binding on all Jews about the year 100 CE.

The chief service the Temple provided was to absolve people of their sins and confirm atonement for the inequity of individuals and the nation as a whole. The service was looked upon as a divine command, without which the people of Israel could not exist. This became the very heart of the Temple cult. None of the prophets conceived the idea of doing away with the sacrificial cult, though some of them looked upon it with disfavor. Rabbi Joshua Benhananya, a levitical singer of the Temple, expressed this idea when he broke forth with his lament: *"Woe unto us that the Temple is destroyed; the place where Israel's sins were atoned. The mourners of Zion use to lament as long as the Temple service existed, the world was blessed because there is no service more precious to God as the service of the Temple".*

It seemed that originally the Morning Prayer was offered at early dawn, even before the morning sacrifice. By the first century of the Common Era the hours of daily prayer as they are known to us today, had been definitely fixed, sometime between 7 and 10 for the Morning Prayer, between 3 and 4 for the afternoon prayers, but there was no exact time assigned for the evening prayer. The Talmud stresses dawn and dusk as the most suitable times for morning and evening prayer. In this connection, we can understand that these ideas came from the Psalms: *"They shall revere thee, while the sun shines and so long as the moon beams, throughout all generations."* And in Psalm 32:6 *"For this let everyone that is godly pray unto thee in a time when thou mayest be found".*

The New Testament mentions the same time for prayers as indicated in Acts 2:15; 10:3; 3:1. The normal hours seem to have been between 9 a.m., 12 to 1 p.m. and late afternoon. While special evening prayers were strongly recommended to Christians, there was no definite regulation for such a service. The Didache prescribed three daily services, without indicating the precise hours. Tertullian was the first to recommend a return to the old accepted hours of worship. It is significant that he based his argument upon scriptural passages taken from the Psalms, which became the most important part of early Christian worship. In the monasteries of the fourth century one regularly encounters prayer offered 7 times daily, distributed during the 24 hours of day and night. The authority for this procedure is based upon reference again in the Psalms 119:164: *"7 times a day do I praise Thee, because of Thy righteous ordinances."* These 7 periods of prayer later became the norm for Roman Catholic Monastic life, and for many it continues to the present day. The contemporaries of Jesus knew various categories of prayer, which were established during the tannaitic age, between 100 BCE and 200 CE. The apostle Paul having been a disciple of the great sage, Rabbam Gamaliel, was familiar with them, though he does not mention all of them. Prayers of praise and exhalations were most esteemed, then expressions of thanksgiving; then the individual personal supplications were lowest in rank of importance.

Besides these three categories, taken over by the church, there were doxology prayers, professions of faith, and all other prayers, now common to both faiths. It must be remembered that Jesus as a child of the synagogue must have known this "Liturgy," although at his time it was not a fixed "liturgy" as we know it today. While there was much freedom in the service of the synagogue at the time of Jesus, it was more rigid in form than we observe today. There was a set of prayers called amidia, which was pronounced standing and certain passages accompanied by a Jewish form of genuflection. Folding the hands in submission to God's will was likewise an old Jewish gesture, as was stepping back after the completion of a prayer, a mark of respect when taking leave of a superior. The amidia was usually recited silently and afterwards repeated aloud by the reader or cantor for those unable to read. The worshiper was permitted to insert private and spontaneous prayers or petitions in certain places, but only on regular workdays.

Much emphasis was laid at that time upon regular daily attendance at the services in the synagogue. Some went to the extreme by asserting that the prayers of man are accepted only in a synagogue. Yet, there was not full agreement on this practice.

The obligation to attend public services three times a day was met with opposition. We find a statement that *"God said to Israel, when you pray, then pray in the*

synagogue, but if you cannot attend the synagogue, then
pray in your fields; and if you cannot worship in your fields,
then pray in your house. However, if you are hindered from
doing that, then pray while lying in your bed, then if you are
prevented from doing that, then meditates in your heart." It
was Rav Kahana who did not practice attending the services
in the synagogue as he felt he needed to do so privately.
Rav Hisda declared that the house of study is more
important than the house of prayer. Some came to study
even during the services. Rabbi Judah is reported that he
would pray only once in 30 days. Upon returning from a
journey, Samuel's father would not pray for three days.
Rav was of the opinion that whoever is upset ought not to
pray. On the whole however, Babylonian Jews were
praised for their regular attendance at public services in the
synagogue.

There were also differences of opinions among the
rabbis in regard to fixed prayer texts. Such men as Rabbi
Joshua, Rabbi Akiva, and Rabbi Eleaclar were among those
who preferred a free outpouring of the soul; they believed
that whoever makes his prayers fixed, his prayers are no
longer acceptable. Rabbi Eleazar said that to pray every day
was to pray an improvised prayer.

In fact, even the fixed forms of prayers remained in
a loose state for many centuries. In the amidiah, only the
first and the last three benedictions were definitely fixed,
while the intermediary time was a frame into which the
people could formulate their own prayers.

The custom to compose prayers to order, never
became prevalent in Jewish "liturgy"; the one instance in
which Rabbam Gamaliel ordered prayers to be composed
may be taken as an exception. The "liturgy" grew through
the continuous improvisations of religious fervor in
moments of inspiration. A select group of men used to
create prayers for their private devotion; and only after

their compositions found favor in the eyes of the people, were they gradually incorporated into public worship. It took more than 900 years of continuous growth for the "liturgy" to reach the state as presented in the first prayer book compiled by Rav Amram in the year 875 CE.

A difference of prayers developed for those who lived in the land of Israel from those who lived in the land of Babylonian. Each had their own set of prayers and each had their own customs and ceremonies.

The difference in the "liturgy," that existed between the Israel and Babylonian traditions was of a more fundamental character than merely textural variation; it touched the very principals of "liturgy" itself. These differences were as follows: In Israel the reading of the Torah, or the Pentateuch, was completed in three years only. In Babylonia it was celebrated annually. In Israel, the people who were called up to read from scripture would read the portion themselves, while in Babylonia a special reader was in charge, called the Bal Koreh, and the people who were called upon would merely listen and recite the blessings as they still do today. In Israel, the amidah consisted of 18 benedictions; in Babylonia it was 19 benedictions. In Israel, 7 and even 6 adults were sufficient to constitute a quorum for public service. In Babylonia 10 adults were required.

All in all, 73 differences were to have existed in the religious customs of Israel and Babylonia. Yet the Babylonian tradition, maintained the strongest hold for the time came when the majority of Jews lived in Babylonia. The Babylonia tradition took complete hold and became a fixed form of "liturgy," still practiced today. There were always differences of opinions regarding private prayers and there were mystics in Israel and Babylonia who developed other customs, reflecting a growing mystical tradition.

When one studies the early literature of the prayer service of both the synagogue and the early church, one is struck with the fact that both used the Psalms as their basic prayer book. Both believed in congregational participation and responsive reading that became part of the tradition of the synagogue and the early church. Each developed its own "liturgy" and each found certain prayers to be a central part of their spiritual experience.

For both the early church and the synagogue, the "liturgy" was based upon the Hebrew Bible. Not only is it saturated with Biblical content and tone, with its ideas and ideals, but whole sections of the Bible are directly incorporated in the "liturgy." The readings from the prophets, and the readings from the book of Psalms made up the very heart of both services. The most important tradition of both the early church and synagogue was that there is a bridge between the two and that bridge is music. The synagogue developed certain basic melodies and tunes, which also became part and parcel of the chanting in the early church. The practice of antiphonal singing was adopted by the early church as it grew out of the synagogue. The fact that one would chant and the congregation would respond became the norm for both traditions.

The early church adopted much of its music from the synagogue because the music from the synagogue sounded like it belonged in worship while the music of Greece and Rome did not appear conducive to the spiritual needs of people. Though the melodies may have changed, the basic root tonal qualities remain the same. We find in the early church many of the melodies the synagogue had sung for generations. We begin to realize that in the very beginning the early church was a form of synagogue worship. It adopted basic prayers, psalms, scriptural readings and melodies. Both reflected a common heritage.

CHAPTER FOUR
Synagogue and early Church articles of Faith

1)   **Understanding Salvation in the early Church**
                        and Synagogue

The principal source of our knowledge about Jesus
are found in the Synoptic Gospels. It appears that the
specific ideas of Jesus' vicarious death are lacking in the
stratum of original Synoptics (Mark, Matthew and Luke).
It may be significant that when one studies the Synoptic
Gospels, Jesus' incarnation is not expressly mentioned and
that in the Gospel of Mark, Jesus' significant birth is totally
absent. Mark mentions Jesus' resurrection without
describing it. The other three Gospels bring different
descriptions of their account of the resurrected Lord. Both
the differences in accounting and the lack of so important an
aspect of Jesus' mission, as reflected by the circumstances
surrounding his special birth, lead a number of more liberal
Christian scholars and rank and file Jewish scholars to view
this material as having been added theological information
that the established church wanted to codify from its
unique warehouse of stories. The growing Greek influence,
as evidenced by Stoic and Neoplatonic positions, provided
the church with accepted philosophical beliefs it felt
comfortable including, once it had moved away from its
original Jewish associations and into the world of Greek
thought and Roman jurisprudence.

The question of the Messianic self-consciousness of
Jesus is difficult to answer, not only because of Jesus
himself, but also because of the obscurities in the source
material. For instance, from studying the source materials
we learn how difficult it is to separate what Jesus said of
himself from those things that were said about him. In those
circles of formulated Synoptic traditions, Christology did

not have the importance that it had in "Pauline Christianity" and the later church. However, while it would seem probable, it is my considered opinion that Christology was not invented as an answer to the delay of the Second Coming: Christological motifs of a return are almost all present in some way in the early Synoptic traditions. Paul, for whom the present salvation by Christ was so central, lived in the strong expectation of his Second Coming. The Book of Revelation, itself an expression of great hope for the Eschatological future, contains a developed Christology. Its author was likely a Hebrew speaking Jewish / Christian. Nor was this type of Christology originally an exclusive product of Hellenistic Christianity. It appears to have originally developed in different Jewish / Christian circles and from those circles in which the synoptic tradition was formed.

It would seem a reasonable assumption that in Jewish / Christian groups in which the idea of salvation through Jesus' incarnation, death and resurrection was itself weak or existed only partially, the longing for the Second Coming would be stronger. That is because salvation had not taken place in a past time but needed to be awaited in a future time. Unfortunately, the documentation about the Messianic hopes of various Jewish / Christian groups in the first century is poor and incoherent. Even so, we now possess sufficient references to show that the situation was more complex than one could have imagined. Until recently, the only Jewish / Christian group known from this period, was the Ebionite Sect, a group of believers who would become outlawed by a legally established church as heretical. They would survive with the Diaspora by living on the fringes of the newly formed Byzantine Empire.

Sam Pines discovered an Arabic Treatise written about the year 1000 CE, and revealing a Jewish / Christian source. While dating from 1000 CE, the greater part of its material comes from the early centuries of Christianity. The source material found in the Arabic Treatise reflects the tradition and opinions of a Jewish / Christian Sect, somewhat different from the Ebionites and very probably identical with the same Nazarenes associated with several church fathers. As modern day Jews, we are grateful to *Sam Pines* for his discovery, for it makes it historically clear that the Ebionites and Nazarenes agreed on some common points. They affirm that Jesus' main function was as a prophet and not the long sought Messiah. The Ebionites did see Jesus as a "true prophet," a kind of Messiah. They believed that the coming of a true Prophet, whom they thought of as being Jesus, abolished the old temporal three powers of: "contemporary prophecy, the existing kingdom and the Aaronic priesthood." This true prophet was believed to have appeared before in different human incarnations throughout history, in fact, from the very beginning of the world. It may appear contentious to distinguish prophetic roles in light of the Christian development of "Christos," the Pauline Messiah who comes for all people, and even transforms creation itself. That is not my purpose here. The purpose of introducing the Nazarenes and reintroducing the Ebionites is to confirm two intermediary groups that stood between fully developed Christianity and traditional Judaism and who took from both, yet were not fully either.

None of the special Ebionite doctrines were professed by the original authors of the Nazarene Text, but the Nazarene Text appears to view Jesus similarly as a significant prophetic person. The concept of Jesus as the special prophet of his day appeared in the first generation of Jesus' disciples. Hints of this view can be found in the Gospels themselves. Even Jesus refers to himself as a prophet in Luke 13:33. The question of Jesus seeing himself only as a prophet, or as the long expected Messiah, no doubt is open to question depending on which faith community one belongs to, but some room remains to raise issues of legitimate variations about how those earliest believers viewed this man Jesus.

The Jewish community, along its liberal lines, believes Jesus to be a prophetic figure caught up in politically violent times and Roman oppression. The Christian community understands him as accepting his special Messianic role to the point of fulfilling its sacrificial limits for the sake of humankind. It would appear that, of those who followed Jesus, either as closely aligned friends or more distant listeners, different understandings of his ministry and historic role have surfaced. The Ebionites and the Nazarenes, both very early Jewish / Christian groups, each had a view of Jesus different than the one mostly demonstrated by the Institutional Church of today. At least the discovery of their belief positions allows open minded people of both faiths to appreciate how theology has developed from earlier historic events and cultural / philosophic influences. Scholarship and careful study of original materials contributes to this view and thus may allow each to have their space.

It can be accepted that such early Christian groups as the Ebionites and the Nazarenes, did not accept the Christology developed by the apostle Paul and consequently did not subscribe to the later official doctrines of the Church. For these groups, the expectation of the Second Coming was primarily centered in someone who would bring political redemption, rather than universal salvation to the entire world.

There are a group of scholars today who maintain that the belief in Jesus as Messiah was created by the vision of the resurrection. Certainly, seeing someone alive who was presumed dead would enliven and confirm a faith, weakened by the catastrophe of a crucifixion. From the

Jewish perspective it should be remembered that the idea of a Messiah who would rise from death and then ascend to heaven is itself foreign. The idea of immediate resurrection and ascension did exist among Jews, for it was by no means a proven test or complementary to Messianic dignity. There is no historic Hebrew account that resurrection will be the crown and consequence of a martyr's death. It is also improbable that Jesus' resurrection was interpreted in the same way that a later Christology would interpret it. Historically, there is no reason that early Christian groups should understand the vision of the resurrected Jesus as a decisive Christological event. It was originally more natural to see in the visions of Jesus as risen and ascended, parallels to the bodily assumptions of Enoch, Moses, or Jeremiah, or to the visions of Elijah, or even the resurrection of the New Testament figure of John the Baptist.

For a Jewish / Christian group to see Jesus as a dead prophet risen by the hand of God, a corresponding progressive weakening of an Eschatological reckoning would occur. That is essentially what happened to the Nazarene sect when it came into conflict with the Church. The Church, though not greatly interested in Eschatology at the time, saw in the Messianic dignity of Jesus and his resurrection, important components to a Christological drama whose final stage would be the Second Coming of Christ. The Nazarenes, like the other Jewish / Christian groups, opposed the established Christology of the Church. That would explain why the resurrection of Jesus is never mentioned in the Nazarene source material. It seems even more probable that according to this Jewish / Christian source, Jesus pronounced his last instructions to his disciples, not after his resurrection, but before. The group's Eschatological hope becomes clear in their sectarian form of the Lord's Prayer. *"Our Father that art in the heavens and the earth. Nothing you demand is beyond your power and nothing that you wish is withheld from you. Forgive us our sins and trespasses and do not punish us in hell."*

As can be seen, the text of the prayer is so changed that even the slightest possibility of a hope for a future is radically eliminated. At a certain stage of their development, the Nazarenes not only weakened, but practically abolished the Eschatological hope of a Second Coming.

The position of the Ebionites, as we can see from their doctrines, was different. Their dynamic belief in a true prophet who appeared in various human forms throughout history, from Adam to Jesus, tended to accept a Second Coming. Indeed, at the end of the first century, a group called the Elchasaites arose among the Ebionites. Their name is derived from the Aramaic Elxai, translated as "the hidden power." The name fits the typical Ebionite belief of successive incarnations of the heavenly power in human form. The Elchasaites thought that this power was at the beginning incarnated in Adam and finally in Jesus (**Editor's Note**: People familiar with the Edgar Cayce readings may recognize this belief from trance pronouncements he made about Jesus). The Elchasaites brought forth a new doctrine that envisioned Jesus as the last hidden power of God, foreseen from the beginning of creation as the God sponsored plan to bring souls back to the Father. The succession of lives from Adam to Jesus paved the way for anyone else to make the same journey. Both the Ebionites and the Nazarenes believed in Jesus' resurrection by the power of God. That puts them closer to main-line Christianity than to main-line Judaism. At the same time they held to other time honored Jewish traditions that identified them as Jews.

The belief in the coming of a new and great power was not something special to early Christianity. We find it especially in the attitude of the Essenes. It is clear from the

Dead Sea Scrolls that this Jewish sect remained faithful to its fervent hope in a national salvidic future. However, they came to conclude that this wicked time would continue longer than the Biblical prophets had foretold. The end of this period was hidden from these ancient teachers, but revealed to the Teacher of Righteousness, the founder of their sect. Essene Eschatology provided a future hope based upon several considerations: (1) the doctrine of double predestination; (2) the members of the community, (3) the belief that the Sons of Light, or God's elect, were preordained for final redemption, while the Sons of Darkness would be destroyed. The dualistic theology of election and curse, together with the strict organization of the sect, led to the view that the Sons of Light, chosen by God's providence, are in a state of grace from the moment they were accepted into the community. Upon entering, it was believed, they received the gift of the Holy Spirit.

From these positions, the Essenes developed a profound anthropology expressing itself in the Thanksgiving Psalms; and the notion that unredeemed humanity is in the sphere of sinful flesh, while the elect can overcome the sins of the flesh with the help of the spirit granted to them. It is clear from this thinking that such anthropology does not strictly need a redemption of the future, for the function of such a redemption of the future can only be complete when salvation has truly occurred. Indeed, it is a fact that the thanksgiving scroll, a political aspect of the final struggle between the Sons of Light and the Sons of Darkness, was not present. The Eschatological events described could only occur in a cosmic happening, a conviction that never left them as their struggle with Rome closed in upon the community.

During the years in which the sect existed, the Essenes believed salvation would come in three stages:

(1st) was a pre-ordained election,

(2nd) was an actual operation of grace, which would begin at the moment when the elect entered the community, and

(3rd) with the Eschatological redemption taking place in a future with its rewards for those who were part of the elect.

It is probable that early Christian trends based on the theologies of John the Evangelist, Paul and the authors of most of the other New Testament Epistles were deeply influenced by these Essene ideas. It is no wonder that the theologies of these important New Testament figures follow the trends of the three Essene stages of redemption. It was especially the Second Stage that received a new meaning for Christian beliefs; namely, *"the grace of salvation of a Christian is caused by faith in Christ's expiation of sins through his death and resurrection."* This belief came into the church a little later as the center of the message, as it was already the main them of Paul's preaching. Thus, there were at the very beginning important groups, who believed that the act of salvation takes place in a recent past through the actions of the person of Jesus. Paul's attitude shows that in such groups the hope for an immanent second coming of Christ could be as strong as it was in other Christian groups who did not stress Christology or even in those groups where Christology did not exist. Paul's witness shows that the developed Christology did exist in the first decades after Jesus' death in some form, but its structure proves that this belief did not emerge as a consequence of a Second Coming.

Not only Paul, but also the Book of Revelation illustrates that Christology can be compatible with the ardent desire for a future redemption. Both the Ebionites and the Nazarenes lacked a belief in salvation as performed by the death and resurrection of Christ. But they too believed in a future Second Coming. The religious movement known as Christianity originated in the hope of a second return. Some thought of Jesus as a special Prophet; but for most, Jesus was the true Messiah who fulfilled the hope of redemption in a past moment and in a future redemption to come.

2)   **Remembering Martyrs through Psalms and Scripture**

The early church and synagogue had a tradition of not forgetting those martyrs who gave their life for the faith. We find, for example, that all of the Christian feasts and special days had Psalms attached to them as well as readings from the New Testament. For example it was to be remembered that on Wednesday before Easter, the early church read from the Book of Job, Chapter 1 and 2 and recited Psalms 79. During Christmas they would read from the Old Testament book of Isaiah 53:8 and would sing Psalms 85. and from the Gospel of Luke 2:1-39. On Easter day the calendar brought the reading from Isaiah 53 and Acts I and Psalms 146. Thus, we note that the church adopted the old Hebraic practice of using a scriptural reading and a Psalm to commemorate the calendar year and this became part and parcel of Christian tradition. It is still done to this day. The church has its regular calendar developed by certain Psalms and Scripture readings that became part and parcel of their way of life.

This must have been taken over from the synagogue, because already during the time of the second Temple the regular schedule of reading from the Torah and the Prophets began to be scheduled, as well as readings from the various Psalms, which were read on every special holiday. We note that in the Jewish calendar every holiday was celebrated by special readings, for example: Reading the Passover Exodus and then reading form the song of Psalms. We also note that the New Year holiday, Rosh Hashanah, had the readings from the chapter of Genesis 22 and the reading from Samuel, Chapter 1. Thus, the church followed very much in the Hebraic tradition by having every holiday of significance with a scriptural reading and also a Psalm, as a part of the "Liturgy."

Not only were the holidays remembered with special Psalms and readings, but the calendar also observed the remembrance of the Saints and the Martyrs.

The first authentic statement of martyr memorials comes from 155 CE when the Church of Smyrna agreed to celebrate the Day of Saint Polycarp's Martyrdom. Thus, it established the concept that martyr's were to be remembered on special days commemorating their service. The question of veneration of martyrs is also a part of the Hebraic calendar tradition. There was the reading of the Book of Esther, followed by fasting. There was also the reading from various Talmudic passages and certain passages from the Midrash where certain passages were read at certain times.

What is so interesting is that this became a Christian tradition from a prior tradition when Jews remembered those who had been martyred for the cause of their people. This was especially true on the Day of Atonement, Yom Kippur. I recall a eulogy written by a famous rabbi and philosopher, Swadya Gaon of Fayum, who remembered the martyrs who were Massacred by the Romans. All of the verses begin with the words, from Lamentations: *"Remember Oh Lord, what has befallen us, remember the martyrs who gave their lives for us we shall not forget them."*

The tradition of remembering the martyrs thus would become a Christian tradition. The practice of celebrating joyfully the Martyr's death on his birthday was not only a Christian custom, there are certain Jewish traces of such festivities. The outstanding example is still celebrated today upon the 33rd day of the Counting of the Omer, occurring on what is called Lag Be Omer. The anniversary of the death and transfiguration of Rabbi Simeon Bar Yohai is celebrated in Meron Galilee by many thousands of visitors who attend the grave where a festivity is held day and night. It is a vigil with torches, bonfires, cutting the first hairs of a baby, and a good deal of folk dancing. This very popular feast is still very much alive. One must recall that even on the anniversary of Moses' death, traditionally, on the seventh day of Adar, members of a pious fraternity who cared for the dead would remember the death of Moses with a festive banquet arranged for this time.

What is fascinating about both traditions is that both of them were concerned about carrying on the memory of those who gave their lives for the faith. It also became part of the "liturgy" of both synagogue and church. The martyrs were remembered on special holidays and were given special Psalms recited in their memory. The most important fact was that the calendar became a place where the martyrs were remembered and where their names were recited so that their tradition would not be forgotten. We know very little about the services that were held in the early days in honor of a Jewish or Christian martyr. The decisive question for the calendar was that it came in the calendar so that from year to year it would be remembered on a special day.

The one group of Psalms, which played a very strong role in the early church, were the hallelujah Psalms, which were Psalms from 145 to 150. They were recited originally in the synagogue on special holidays, especially on Passover and the Feast of Tabernacles, as well as on Feast of Weeks. They became a regular part of the service.

When we investigate the "liturgy" of the early church, we also note that for all of the major Christian

holidays the hallelujah Psalms were incorporated almost
identically to the way as they were incorporated in the
synagogue. It became a way of giving thanks, something
very popular in Christian churches. We note that the Hallel
Psalms, 145 to 150, were recited on Passover and on Easter
Psalm 118 was recited. Thus, one faith carried over to
another. They were both reciting the same Psalms at
different times, but the same spirit of the Psalms was there.
The synagogue kept a tradition alive by keeping alive the
Psalms and the scripture readings together. The church
followed the same direction by having the same tradition of
reading from scripture and reciting Psalms for every special
holiday tradition, often duplicating the cantilation that was
used in the synagogue.

3) Comparative understanding of the teachings of Jesus and Hillel

One of the great teachers of Judaism was the famous Rabbi
Hillel who lived about 100 years before the birth of Jesus.
It is quite possible that some of his teachings found their
way into Jesus' thinking. When one studies Hillel and the
Talmud one is immediately struck by the fact that Hillel
believed that one should have a positive view of himself.
He should not belittle himself, but should have a sense of
great self-esteem, which for him was most important in
dealing with the problems of life. His influence is quite
profound throughout the Talmud and throughout Jewish
life. He was a man of deep humility, yet at the same time,
emphasized the need for self-assertion and self-esteem.

Of interest to students of the Gospels, it should be
noted that Jesus knew at least one of Hillel's sayings about
his own person. Jesus said: *"But if it is by the finger of God
that I drive out the devils, then be sure that the kingdom of
God has already come upon you - he who is not with me is
against me, and he who does not gather with me scatters."*

(Luke 1120-23). The meaning of this saying is clear enough, *"a moment of revival had begun in Israel and this revival is the realization of the Kingdom of God on earth. But this movement was to be centered around Jesus' person: Separate initiatives, independent of Jews would not be able to gather but to scatter."* (taken from sayings of Hillel)

Others have observed the end of Jesus' sayings are similar to Hillel's famous words, which are preserved in numerous places in Talmudic literature. In Simre Cutta, Hillel's Rarralels words from the first part of Sifre Cutta, and Hillel's parallel words from the first part of a longer passage reads, *"It is time to act for the Lord, they have broken the law"* (Psalm 119:126). You have to read they have broken the law - it is time to act for the Lord. So Hillel: *"in time when men scatter, gather, when there is no demand by them! In the place where there are no men, strive to be a man!"* The first of these three short sentences occurred in other places in Rabbinic literature in expanded form: *"In the time when men gather, scatter; in time when men scatter, gather."* It is difficult to determine whether this larger form was original or secondary. The focus of Hillel's saying is the study of the oral law, which for Hillel was the foundation stone of his faith. His background comes at a time when King Herod the Great was in charge of the kingdom of Judah and not a truly practicing Jew. His father was an Idumenin and his mother was a Novatian. He came to the throne by marrying into the family of the Hasmonans. At the time when Herod was putting forth his great buildings, especially the building of the Temple, he began to emphasis the need to study the law as he saw it. He was trying to win the favor of his people by becoming a great builder. At the same time, the law was being broken. Hillel tries to bring people together for study, by telling the people: *"when men gather, scatter, and when men scatter, gather."* It is obvious from these words that Hillel was worried that studying the law as a group might prove dangerous to many who are pursuing the study of the law. It is interesting to note that Jesus' words *"who does not gather with me, scatters"* expresses very much what Hillel was saying. There are no direct references to Hillel in the New Testament and one cannot find any direct connection to Hillel's teaching except where one is able to find select parallels to Jesus' teachings.

Jesus likely knew Hillel's sayings and may have adapted them to his own situation. While Hillel had spoken about the gathering of the increased bulk of oral tradition, Jesus evidently thought of the gathering of people. A second difference between the sayings of Jesus and Hillel is that while Hillel addresses himself to others, Jesus sees the importance of his own task. Yet, this difference is smaller than it seems at first glance. Where Hillel speaks in the imperative to a general "you" there are also sayings in which he speaks in the first person. For example: *"If I am not for myself, who is for me? When I am for only myself, what am I? And if not now when?"* (Avot 1:14) This saying resembles Jesus' words in the Gospel of Luke: *"He who is not with me is against me"* (Luke 11:23).

4)   The Jewish Roots of a Hellenistic Jew:
Paul of Tarsus

In the study of Paul we note that he boasted of his Jewish origin and with regards to his opponents he would say, *"Are they Hebrews? So am I. Are they Israelites? So am I. Are they of the seed of Abraham? So am I."* (II Cor 11:22). He says emphatically, *"For I am an Israelite of the seed of Abraham, of the tribe of Benjamin".* (Philippians 3:4) Or again he would say in a debate with his opponents; *"If any other man thinks to have confidence in the flesh. I yet more, circumcised the 8th day of the stock of Israel, of the tribe of Benjamin, a Hebrew of Hebrews, as touching the law, a Pharisee."* (Rom 11:1). In his speech before the Sanhedrin in Jerusalem, he is recorded as saying: *"I am a Pharisee, a son of Pharisees"* (Acts 23:6) Here we note that Paul took great pride in his Jewish heritage and in his Jewish tradition. Paul delivered these words to the people of Jerusalem at the time of his arrest: *"I am a Jew, born in Tarsus of Cimica, but brought up in this city, at the feet of Gamaliel, and instructed according to the strict manner of the law of our fathers. Being zealous for God, even as you are all this day."* (Acts 22:3). He always believed that he had a mission to fulfill that drove him each day, but he never forgot that *"we are Jews by nature, and not sinners of the Gentiles!"* (Gal. 2:15). With all his Universalism, three times in successions, he emphatically says: *"To the Jew first, and also to the Greek."* In his great love for the people, he declares: *"For I could wish that I myself were accursed from Christ for my brethren, my countrymen according to the flesh, who are Israelites, to whom pertain the adoption, the glory, the covenants, the giving of the law, the service of God, and the promises; of whom are the fathers and from whom, according to the flesh, Christ came, who is over all, the eternally blessed God. amen".* (Rom. 9:3-5)

When the pagan and Christians congregations began to manifest racial prejudice towards the Jewish Nazarenes who were among them, Paul came out against them in stinging words: *"Israel is a good olive tree and the pagans are a wide olive tree which has been grafted upon the good olive tree."* (Rom. 10-5). Israel for him was the root and the pagans were the branches which grew out from the trunk; the branches. The chief element is the believing Israel and not the believing pagans; therefore, the pagan Christians have no right to despise the Jewish Nazarenes. For in the end God will fulfill his promise, delivered by the prophets, and the sons of Israel will be saved. From the heart of a Jew gone astray, yet loving his people, he cried out of his being: *"Brothers, my heart's desire, and my supplication to God is for them, that they may be saved. For I bear them witness that they have a zeal for God, but not according to knowledge."*(Rom 10:12)

Even at the end of his life, after he had had many sharp conflicts with Jews, and they had punished him a number of times with 40 lashings, lacking one, and even attempted to stone him to death; and even after he had been taken prisoner to Rome with the accusations of the Jews of Jerusalem upon him - after all of this, he called from his place of confinement,the Jews of Rome and assured them that he had no accusations against his people.

Paul never felt himself a non-Jew, in spite of the fact, that in moments of bitterness, when he was being persecuted by the Jews or the Nazarenes, he would forget the Christian love to which he sang such a glorious hymn of praise, and then speak harshly about the Jews or even curse them with violent curses. (I Thess.2: 14-6) On such occasions, he would make a statement about whether the Jews had a covenant and the promise, and would declare that because the Jews did not believe in Jesus as messiah, they were no longer God's first born sons, Israel, but that the birthright had been taken from them and given to believing Gentiles.

Yet, we feel that even in his moments of anger, he speaks of Israel as he does out of the consciousness of his love for Israel and out of his desire to be of the first born of God who should accept faith in Jesus. If someone had suggested to Paul that he cease being a Jew, he not only would not have agreed to this, but he would not even have understood such a suggestion. He always saw Christianity according to his own conception of it, namely, that it was true Judaism; and he considered that he was bringing the Gentiles into this Judaism and not taking the Jews out of

Judaism. Paul was mistaken in thinking this. Actually, he lead the Jews believing in Jesus out of Judaism and after a time he easily inducted them into a kind of compromising half paganism, but he was not aware of this. I do not believe he intended to do it. He never imagined that this would be the way things would turn out. His Christianity was a new and improved kind of Judaism, something like the Essenes, for example, except that in this new Judaism it was possible and necessary to include the Gentiles and therefore it was proper for this Judaism to be distinguished from the old and unbelieving Judaism by a special type of congregation made up of both believing Jews and believing Gentiles. But he did not see or understand that this distinction would, of necessity, bring into being an essentially new religion, one which would have only a portion of Judaism and thus would not be true historic Judaism at all. How could a disciple of Rabbi Rabban Gamaliel the elder, have thought otherwise? Truly, Paul was a Jew not only in his physical appearance, but in his thinking and in his entire inner life. For Paul, he was not only "*a son of Pharisees*," he was also one of those disciples of the Talmud who, brought up on the study of Torah, did not cease to cherish it to the end of his days. It would be difficult to find a more typical Talmudic exposition of Scripture than what you discover in the Epistles of Paul.

Here is a typical example: *"But the righteousness which is of faith says thus, say not in their heart who shall ascend into the heavens (that is to bring Christ down) or who shall descend into the abyss? That is to bring Christ up from the dead. But what sayeth it? The word is nigh in thy mouth and in thy heart: that is the word of faith which we preach: because if thou shall confess with thy mouth, Jesus as Lord, and shall believe in thy heart that God raised him from the dead, thy shall be saved: for he who with the heart of man believeth unto righteousness and with the mouth makes*

confession is made unto salvation. For scripture says, 'Whosoever believeth on him shall not be put to shame' ".
(Rom. 10:6-11) Paul here changes one part from the Pentateuch to suit his own needs and in place of: *"who shall go over the sea for us,"* he substitutes another scriptural passage, drawing from it the conclusions desired and needed by him, even though there is no hint of them in the passage itself. Continuing, he supports his interpretation with a verse from the Prophets, although in the Greek Bible, the Septuagint, this verse lacks the words for him. In place of the reading, *"shall not be put to shame,"* the Hebrew has the words, *"he shall not make haste."*

There is another example where he states: *"Now to Abraham, where the promise is spoken, and to his seed. He says not ' and to seeds as of many, but as of one, and to thy seed which is Christ."* One might assume Paul did not know that seed is a collective noun, the plural number of which does occur in the Hebrew. It occurs in the Talmud where we find a plural of seeds. Is this not typically a Talmudic debating devise where one finds the words which would fit the interpretation one sought to make?

In yet another example of Paul's method of discourse we find: *"For it is written in the Law of Moses thou shalt not mussel the ox when he treads out the corn. Is it for the oxen that God cares, or does he say altogether for our sake? Yeah, for our sake, it was written because he that plows, or to plow and hope, and he that threshes, or to thresh in hope of partaking the products of plowing and threshing. If we sowed unto you Christians spiritual things, is it a great matter if we shall reap your carnal things?"*
(I Cor. 9: 9-11) Here in this example the real meaning of the commands *"Thou shalt not mussel... thou shall mussel the ox when he tread the corn"* is not the simple literal meaning. It would be cruelty to animals, if the ox is not allowed to eat some of the grain which it has threshed. God forbid that

the matter should be that simple. Is it for the oxen that God cares? No, rather the ox is the preacher of the Gospel who sows spiritual things among the Christians and his interpretation of : *"Thou shalt not mussel the ox,"* is that it is forbidden to deny the sower of spiritual things the right of obtaining carnal things, which means financial support from congregants, since even Jesus himself did ordain, *"They that proclaim the Gospels shall live form the Gospels."* Here again we see a typical Jewish form of interpretation in which Paul then goes to use his analogy in order to prove his point. An important part of his teaching, was the fact that he believed very strongly that one could read scripture and then interpret it according to one's knowledge and background and experience. Here Paul used his knowledge and background to always interpret it according to the way he had been taught at the feet of the great master, Rabban Gamaliel. He sought an interpretation that came from what he saw in himself, one which he felt belonged to both Jew and non-Jew. We know that as a student he probably did speak Hebrew or a Jewish Aramaic and yet all his writings are in Greek, in spite of all the Hebrew he had learned. He lived in Jerusalem a number of years and visited Jerusalem many times; yet he returned to Tarsus in the prime of his life and stayed there 8 years. Could it have been possible for a talented and perceptive man like Paul not to have been influenced by the pagan culture of Tarsus, his native city? For thirty years or more he carried on journeys in foreign states, passing through all the great and extensive Roman Empire except Egypt, which was inhabited chiefly by Pagan Gentiles.

To be sure, Paul the Apostle, did not formerly study Greek learning, but in terms of his background and tradition, he had received an excellent Greek education and he thought and wrote in this language and felt close to it as it was native to his heart and to his belief. At the same time

105

he always proclaimed that he was a Jew of the Diaspora, a Jew of the exile and in this sense he was detached from authentic living Judaism, which was rooted in its own cultural soil. He lived and directed his life in the Greek community and therefore one finds a kind of ambiguity between what he felt, what he said and what he did. Intensive research over the years has proven that Paul, in his teachings, did find his roots in his faith, but then sought to extend that faith beyond its borders, using it consciously to create a new kind of religion, a religion which would eventually divorce itself from Judaism and become a part of a new faith and tradition.

5) **Peter and the Manual of Discipline**

The New Testament Epistles are really based upon earlier Christian Sermonic pieces, linked together by the authors of these Epistles. As we study these Epistles we cannot help but see that there are many parallels with the Dead Sea Scrolls. In particular, we notice a most fascinating parallel between First Peter 2:5-6 with a passage in the Essene manual of discipline 8:4-10.

We read in the manual of discipline: *"A house of holiness for Israel and a foundation of the holy of holies for Aaron to offer pleasant fragrance and they shall be acceptable for this is the tested wall, a corner stone of great worth, if its foundation will not tremble or move from their place."* In a passage in First Peter 2:5-6 we read the following: *"Come let yourself be built as living stones into a spiritual house to become a holy priesthood to offer spiritual offerings acceptable to God through Jesus Christ. For it stands in scripture: Behold I am lain in Zion a tested stone, a cornerstone of great worth and he who believes in him shall not be put to shame."*

The literary connection between Peter and the Essene Manual Discipline is very clear and precise. The main difference between the two texts is in the understanding of the end of Isaiah 28:16. While the Manual of Discipline interprets these words in a sermonic way we find that First Peter quotes the Greek Bible and uses the terminology: *"And he who believes in him shall not be put to shame."* These words are explained in First Peter as: *"The great worth of which it speaks is for you who believe, but for those who do not believe these very stones which the builder rejected have become the chief cornerstone* (Psalms 118:22) *and a stone to trip over, a rock of stumbling* (Isaiah 8:14); *for they stumble, for they disobey the words, as they were destined to do."*

The stone referred to in First Peter is the Christ: *"Come to him, to that living stone rejected by men but in God's sight is chosen and of great worth."* Here First Peter already alludes to both Psalm 118:22 and Isaiah 28:16 We note here how this verse was used also in the Manual of Discipline as well as by First Peter. According to Luke 20:18 Jesus said: *"Everyone who falls upon that stone shall be broken; but on whomsoever it shall fall it will grind him to powder."* The view of First Peter is that the stone Christ has an opposite function for those who believe in him and a same function towards those who do not believe in him. The contrast is depicted by two quotations taken from Isaiah: *"For the believers, Christ is the cornerstone of great worth."* (from Isaiah 28:16) *but for those who do not believe in him he becomes a stone to stumble upon."* The same contrast is expressed in Simon's word in Luke 2:34-35 namely that: *"Jesus is set for the fall and the rising of many in Israel, and for a sign that is spoken against - that thoughts out of many hearts may be revealed."*

How fascinating it is that the Manual of Discipline also speaks of the stone as a test, as a test for the truth. We find the very same thing in First Peter where Christ is a stone for him which tests those who come to him; for those who believe, he becomes a stone to trip over and a rock that causes men to stumble. It is most interesting to compare a similar interpretation of Isaiah 28:16 from the medieval Jewish commentator Rabbi Isaiah Ben Malidi Trani who lived around the time 1260 CE when he said: *"In Zion a stone as a stone to trip over a testing stone, as there the wicked shall be tested and this stone shall be a great cornerstone of great worth and similar to this as it will become the head of the corner."* The medieval rabbi even combines 28:16 with the same Old Testament verse, which appears in First Peter. Thus, First Peter uses the term in its heretic sense and it must have been that he was influenced by the Essene way of thinking. The author of the Thanksgiving Scroll, (6:26-28) describes his community as *"testing stones to build a wall of strength that will not tremble; all who enter it shall never be moved, for no strangers shall come into its doors."* While the motif is not identical, the content of the words are similar to what is used in First Peter 2:7-9.

Until the present, from the Scrolls that have been published, we have not found the precise idea of a sect being a testing wall, or considered being head of the corner for the elect ones, or as a stone to trip over -a rock of stumbling for the damned ones, who do not believe. However, the general concept fits Essene thought and their symbolic views. It is possible that, like the preceding verses in First Peter 2:5-9, this is an adaptation of an Essene text, which in its new form no longer speaks about the community, but about Christ who has become the primary subject of the passage. It is possible that the supposed Jewish text was part of the Essene source which is behind First Peter 2:5-6. I believe there was a relationship between the author of First Peter and the author of the Thanksgiving Scroll.

CHAPTER FIVE
Comparing practices of the early
Church and Synagogue

1)   **Food Symbolism in Synagogue and Church**
Food was a powerful manifestation of God's
presence, for the power of the Lord is manifested in his
ability to control food; to feed is to bless, to confer life; to
feed bad food or to starve is to judge or punish or actually
to confer death.

Food was a way of talking about the law and
lawlessness. It dated at least to the Babylonian exile in the
mid sixth century, b.c.e. when the Pentateuch and
Deuteronomic books are estimated to have taken their final
form.

In understanding the tradition of food, we need to
understand that acceptance of the power and authority of
God is symbolized by acceptance of his food. The
rejection however, of the power and authority of the Lord
is symbolized by seeking after food he has forbidden.

The people limit or tempt the Lord, that is to
question the extent of his power or authority, by
questioning his ability to feed them. God's word is equated
with food. Eating enjoins people with God or separates
them from the Lord.

The power and authority of God is manifested in
his ability to control food and therefore, to bless. In the
Pentateuch, God's commandments signify his personal
activity, a virtue which still exists in the universe. God, the
Master of the entire world, is conceived as operating
through his word, is conceived as operating through his
word. At once the expression of his will and his execution
period. His command is the underlying principle of all
creation, all orderliness in the quest of nature. History is

providential because God may give or withhold as he alone chooses.

God's first command on creating living beings and putting them in their places defines the food *"which they will persist or perish."* Thus, in Psalm 194, we notice this in the psalmist praise of God; *"O Lord how manifold are thy works! In wisdom have You made them all; the earth is full of Your creatures. These all look to Thee, to give food in due season. When You give it to them, they gather it up, and when You open Your hands they are filled with good things. When You hide Your face, they are dismayed; when You take away their breath, they die and return to the dust. When You send forth Your spirit, they are created, and You renew the faith of the ground."*

God's creation proceeds through a series of recreations, distinguished by the foods His new creatures may or may not eat. Thus, Adam and Eve in Eden may eat everything of the garden except the fruit of the tree of knowledge of good and evil (Genesis 2:16-17). But when they eat the forbidden fruit and are cast out, they must eat *"the plants of the fields"* bread and sweat of their faces, for *"cursed is the ground because of you"*. *"In toil you shall eat of it all the days of your life"* (Genesis 3:17-18).

Noah and his seed, the remnant saved from the flood, may eat all things except meat with blood in it. *"Every moving thing that lives shall be food for you and as I gave you the green plants, I give you everything. Only you shall not eat flesh with a life that is its blood."* (Genesis 9:3-5). The children of Israel, passed over by the angel of death in Egypt, are instructed to eat the Passover meal, which represents in its food, and in the manner of its consumption, their salvation at the hands of the Lord. The Passover is forbidden to the foreigner (Exodus 12). The children of Israel are delivered in the wilderness. God's gift of water from an imposing rock (Exodus 17), they are told to store in a vessel on the altar as a sign of His divine power. *"I see you in the wilderness where I brought you out of the land of Egypt"* (Exodus 16:32). Canaan is the land he promised them, *"a land flowing with milk and honey."* When they arrived they were instructed first of all in the dietary rules. *"This is the law pertaining to beast and bird and every living creature that moves throughout the waters and every creature that swarms upon the earth, to make a distinction between the clean and the unclean, between the living creatures that may be eaten and the living creatures that may not be eaten"* (Leviticus 11:46-47).

The Lord stands by His children in adversity: *"Thou prepares a table before me in the presence of mine enemy"* (Psalm 23:5). Jerusalem that the Lord has restored to the Jews, following the exile from Babylon, will nourish them like a mother with the wealth of nations: *"Behold, I will extend prosperity to her like a river and the wealth of nations like an ever flowing stream"* (Isaiah 66:11-12). Nourishment is an important feature of worldly nations. The same metaphor is used of human political leaders to symbolize the power and authority over the people.

Early Christian writers relied on these images to represent the divine power and authority of Jesus. The multiplication of the loaves and fishes is recounted six times: twice by Matthew and Mark, once each by Luke and John. Carry the church; cherish the memory of it, because it was a very deep part of their experience of Jesus. Jesus' feeding miracles paralleled the scriptural stories of the Passover and God's miraculous gift of manna in the wilderness (John 6:4). Jesus gives the same command to his disciples that the Lord gave to Saul and David: "Feed my sheep".

In the Gospel of John, we read this interesting story: *"When they had finished breakfast, Jesus said to*

111

*Simon, son of John, Simon, do you love me more than thee?
And Simon said, Yes Lord, you know that I love you, and
Jesus said to him, feed my lambs. A second time he said,
Simon, son of John, 'Do you love me?' Simon once again
said to him, 'Yes, Lord, you know that I love you', and Jesus
said, 'tend you my sheep'''.*

Paul feeds his companions on what he predicted
would be a disastrous ship voyage, and then they escaped
their captors and reached land safely (Acts 27:33-38). He
feeds his flock of Corinthians as *"babes in Christ"* with
milk, not solid food to equate them gradually with the
Lord's wisdom (1 Corinthians 3:1). The Lord often has to
seek out the sheep whom His faithless shepherds do not
feed, but feed on, abused, left to be devoured by wild
beasts.

Thus, Jesus feeds and eats with bad characters to
seek out and save what was scattered and lost. Indeed it is
precisely the hungry, the poor and the persecuted who
Jesus, like the prophets before him, predicts will inherit the
earth. To feed bad food or starve is to judge or punish. It
is inconceivable that God should not feed a faithful flock,
but the faithless deserve different treatment. The Lord's
destructive power is also conveyed through the medium of
food. His treatment of Adam and Eve provides us with an
understanding that paradise was meant for the good, which
the Lord would bring.

In the prophet Isaiah we note how this concept of
food is so important: *"Come now, let us reason together
says the Lord. If you are willing and obedient, you shall eat
the good of the land; but if you refuse and rebel, you shall be
devoured by the sword"* (Isaiah 1:18-20).

Destruction comes as a feast or famine period. The
people of Israel complained to Moses and Aaron in the
desert: *"Would that we had died by the hand of the Lord in
the land of Egypt, when we sat by the flesh pots and ate*

bread to the fullest, for You have brought us into the wilderness to kill this whole assembly with hunger" (Exodus 16:3).

It is interesting to note how God feeds his people and how the cup remains a symbol of that feeding, which God gives unto his people. We see it in the Psalms 116: *"Then you shall say to them, thus says the Lord of hosts, the God of Israel, drink, be drunk and vomit, fall and rise no more, because of the sword I am sending among you. And if they refuse to accept the cup from your hand to drink, then you shall say to them "Thus says the Lord of hosts, you must drink"* (Psalms 75-78).

The cup reappears in early Christian writings where it is turned into Jesus himself. When he finally accepts the Roman soldiers "sour wine" he dies, provoking, according to John, one of the earliest curses in scripture: *"They gave me poison for food and for my thirst they gave me vinegar to drink. Let their own table before them become a snare. Let their sacrificial feast be a trap"* (Matthew 27:48).

Paul cites the curse again in his letter to the Romans: *"Let their table become a snare and a trap, a pitfall, a retribution for them"* (Romans 11:9). Thus, the cup becomes an important symbol for both Jewish and Christian experience. The Jew always raises the cup in terms of every blessing and for the celebration of every holiday, festival and Sabbath period.

The cup also became important in Christian tradition for it was from the cup that when we see the wine, his well has the communion period. Thus, we note how each dependent on the concept of the cup has been an important factor in understanding their relationship to themselves as well as to others.

Acceptance or rejection of the power and authority of God is symbolized by the acceptance or rejection of his food. The psalmist prayed to the Lord *"The Lord is my*

chosen portion and my cup, yea I have a goodly heritage"
(Psalms 16:5-6). One notes also that in the New
Testament, Jesus is no less reluctant to drink the bitter cup.
Three times in the garden of Gethsemane, he prays to God
to take it away: *"Abba, Father, all things are possible to
Thee"*, *"remove this cup from me, yet not my will, but thy
will"* (Mark 14:36). This time God does not relent. Jesus
asks his disciples *"Are you able to drink the cup that I
drink?"* They answered, *"We are able"*, though in the end
they are not. Paul uses the same imagery to condemn
idolatry: *"I do not want to be partners with demons. You
cannot drink the cup of the Lord and the cup of demons.
You cannot partake of the table of the Lord and the table of
demons. Shall we provoke the Lord to jealousy? Are we
stronger than him?"* (Corinthians 10:20-22)

As we study the relationship of food to the early
church, we are finding examples of a Divine and human
behavior. For the first time food that God provides is his
word: The food embodies his wisdom. The second is that
eating God's wisdom should establish a binding agreement,
a covenant among the eaters to abide by his word. The
first of these assumptions is stated explicably in a variety
of ways. The unleavened bread of the Passover, for
example, is intended by the Lord as a sign on your hand and
a memorial between your eyes, that the Lord may be in
your mouth: *"Go with a strong hand. The Lord brought
you out of the land of Egypt"* (Exodus 13:9). God's saving
food in the wilderness is likened to be God's wisdom.
Manna must be preserved in a vessel on the altar in the
Temple to *"make you know that man does not live by bread
alone, but man lives by everything that proceeds out of the
mouth of the Lord"* (Deuteronomy 8:3). Both the manna
and the rock were called God's wisdom. The association of
wisdom with food underlies many of the passages in
scripture. Thus, gathering together to pray was also a time

to share in food. For food was symbol of communication and bond.

In the New Testament, Jesus preaches almost the same message: *"Blessed are those who hunger and thirst after righteousness for they shall be satisfied".* Jesus quotes Deuteronomy in response to the Devil who tempts him while he is fasting in the wilderness. He tells his disciples to beware of the leaven of the Pharisees, although they become confused and think he is speaking of bread and not ideas. They have just come from the multiplication of the loaves and fishes and have forgotten to take any of the leftover with them. He also cautions them against false prophecy, which he compares to thorns masquerading as grapes.

Jesus was not concerned with the dietary laws, for he did not specify exactly what he meant by obeying the commands of clean food. The Pharisees may have regarded themselves as living embodiments of the Lord but for Christians, Jesus is the only true prophet because he feeds his people on the truth when in John he says to them, *"I am the living bread which came down from Heaven; If anyone eats from this bread, he will live forever, and the bread which I shall give for the life of the world is my flesh"* (John 6:51). The consequence of eating God's word is the covenant, the creator of all rights and duties in Judaism which one is bound to come and to understand in the words of Isaiah, *"All who are thirsty, come, fetch water, come you who have no food, buy corn and eat; come and get what is not bread, why give the price of your labor and go unsatisfied? Only listen to me and you will have good food to eat and you will enjoy the fat of the land. Come to me and listen to my words, hear me and you shall have life. I will make a covenant with you this time forever to love you faithfully as I have loved David"* (Isaiah 55:1-3).

Thus, we note there was an important part to religious experience in eating the holy food together. This was done not only later in the synagogue during the Passover but also for the Sabbath and for every holiday. There were special foods which became a symbol of the holiday and which played a very important part in terms of their way of life and experience.

Christians who followed Jesus later in the early church began their worship by observing the Lord's feast called the agape. And there they would gather to share in their love and in the giving of food to each other.

The priestly code identified the table of the Lord with the altar of the Jerusalem Temple. But other things have to be understood. That the priestly code also directed one how to keep a truly clean home and to follow the laws regarding the dietary period.

The judge Gideon, who had reason to wonder about God's commitment to the Israelites, doubted the reality of His angels' emissary: *"Pray sir, if the Lord is with us, why then has all of this befallen us? And where are all his wonderful deeds, which our Fathers recounted to us? "* (Judges 6:13). The angel agreed to wait while Gideon got him a present so Gideon prepared him a meal. When the angel, consumed by fire, vanished in the process, Gideon perceived that he was the Angel of the Lord and that he would indeed win against the Midianites with God's help (Judges 6:11-24).

Jesus provides his own test meals to prove the reality of his resurrection to his doubting disciples by transforming breakfast and suppers into sacrificial offerings. When he broke the bread and gave it to them their eyes were open and they recognized him and he vanished out of their sight (Luke 24:31). Recounting their experiences later, they told how he was known to them in the breaking of bread and he appeared again, this time to prove that he was not of the spirit. He urged them to touch him and said *"Have you anything here to eat?"* They gave him a piece of broiled fish and he took it and ate before them. Thus, both the Jews in the Synagogue and the Christians in the early church found a sense of unity as they partook bread together. Breaking bread was a symbol of their unity and love and their regard for each other. For this was the way in which they built a strong bond that became part and parcel of their heritage.

Thus, we note that there was a tremendous union between the heritage of both synagogue and church in the sense that food played a very strong part of that bond. Today it is important to understand and realize that food blessed, whether in the synagogue or the church, became part of the common heritage that was special and unique to both faiths.

2) The Social Message from Qumran to the early Church

The very foundation of Judaism is based on the concept of justice and righteousness for all peoples. Its concept of the unity and its social message became the foundation also of two world religions, Christianity and Islam, developing from its roots. Thus, the social approach from life was not only one of the important causes of the birth of these two great religions, but also through them the Jewish social heritage is still manifested today in modern culture.

Although the importance of the social message of Judaism became a vital part of their legacy, it also must be pointed out that the Greeks and Romans did not have this concept of social justice. Their tradition was entirely different from that of the Jewish people.

The most important source of these ideas of the social message can be found in the Hebrew Bible, which also became the Holy Book, which also became the Holy Book of Christianity. The other source, the New Testament, stems from late Judaism. Ancient Christianity tended to learn from the spiritual achievements of Hellenistic Judaism and the Jewish roots of the teachings of Jesus and of the mother church of Jerusalem are very basic to our understanding of how the church grew and developed from its Jewish roots. The tendency of Christianity, which finds expression, especially in the first three Gospels, reveals a close affinity with a common Jewish non-sectarian tradition, which was then mainly represented by the Pharisees. Their prominent interest in social justice found its way into the Gospel of Jesus and through the New Testament into our own time.

There was also not only in the Hebrew Bible, a tradition of a social message, but also in the ancient scrolls of Qumran in the vicinity of the Dead Sea. Most scholars rightly point out that these are remnants of the literature of an ancient Jewish sect of Essenes, already know from other sources especially from Josephus and from the Greek Jewish Philosopher, Philo.

In antiquity there was the idea of the community of property for which the Essenes were famous for this kind of livelihood and community property became the very foundation stone of their economic life. The existences of this community of property are now confirmed by the scrolls. It is probable that this communal way of life originated in the strict observance of ritual purity by the sects; its members were forbidden to have contact with outsiders. This practice could lead to the maintenance of common warehouses and since coins can transmit ritual impurity, even to the community of wealth. Another source of the Essenes community of wealth was their idealization of poverty. According to their ideology the poor man is closer to God than the rich man. Thus, a member of the sect who has no private property is more acceptable in God's eyes, but the economics of a community way of life of the Essenes was actually based upon their dualistic theology. They believed that humanity is divided by a divine predestination into the blessed lap of God, and into the cursed lap of Belial. Thus, a permanent hatred existed between these two Gentiles. Naturally, this strict belief of the Essenes in a double predestination serves in their dualistic trend in justification for their strong, separatist tendencies. Although we know from Josephus and their own literature that the Essenes outlook led them to become a closed group in the places where they lived. Thus, it was the Essene center to go out and live in the wilderness in Qumran where they would not be corrupted by society. They deeply believed that by doing so they could truly become the elect of God. Consequently the Essene theology was connected with their form of organization and their form of organization was based on a social message that only by justice by righteousness can salvation be truly achieved.

As one studies the New Testament, one becomes convinced that there must have been some connection between the Dead Sea sect and John the Baptist. It seems that John was influenced by the Essene teaching but that he did not remain in the sect because of difference of doctrine. Evidently he declined to accept the view that salvation should be restricted to members of a sect and conditioned by the acceptance of a harsh discipline. According to John the Baptist, there is only one condition fro salvation; Baptism and his theology of Baptism were similar to or even identical with that of the Essenes. Thus, the Baptist did not demand of the persons he baptized that they leave their position in society and separate themselves from their former way of life. In Luke we hear these words: *"The crowd asked him, what shall we do?"* He replied: *"Let everyone who possesses two shirts share with him who has none and let him who has food do likewise."* The Essenes maintained the community of property in a closed sect, while John the Baptist asked his adherents to share their goods with those who are truly poor.

The discovery of the Dead Sea Scrolls have shown that there are Essene elements in Jesus' message, the synoptic Gospels. The Gospels of Matthew, Luke and Mark are the main channel to which the Essene social doctrine had influenced their teachings. It seems that Jesus knew these motifs as they were modified by John the Baptist. Like the Baptist Jesus did not ask his followers to leave their actual social frame and not preach the community of property. All that he said was, that if a man wanted to be perfect, he had to give his property to the poor and follow him. What Jesus wanted from his close group of adherents was not an economic communism but an almost absolute poverty.

The situation however, changed after his death. Community of property was introduced in the mother church of Jerusalem and the description of the institution in the Acts of the Apostles had a great impact upon Christianity even to our own time. It established the concept of the monastic way of life in which community property was part of the community group which lived together and shared completely in all worldly goods.

The Essene influence upon the social structure of the Christian community of Jerusalem can be detected even in the Essene terminology found in the Acts of the Apostles. The influence of this way of life still prevails in the monastic orders of the Roman Catholic Church as well as that of the Greek Orthodox Church.

The ideal of poverty meant for the sect that wealth is an impediment to salvation so its members prayed in the following manner; *"And thou has not placed my support in unjust gain and with wealth, gained by violence my hearts desires not any carnal intent would you have assigned for me."* We note also that they could be closer to God through poverty than through wealth. This was evidently the meaning of the term used by Jesus when he spoke of the poor who are endowed with the Holy Spirit. Jesus thought it is difficult for a rich man to enter the kingdom of heaven. Like the Essenes, Jesus too brought the message of salvation to the poor, the mourners, the persecuted, the meek and the simple. The sect's influence on this ideology of poverty is clear from another saying of Jesus; *"No one can serve two masters. Either he will hate one and love the other, or he will stand by one and despise the other, you cannot both serve God an mammon"* (Matthew 6:24). This saying is not only replete with Essene phraseology but it also reflects its dualistic tendency. We find also in the Christian writings of II Corinthians 6:14-16, *"Keep out of all incongruous ties with unbelievers. What has righteousness and iniquity in common or how can bright associate with darkness? What harmony can there be between Christ and Belial or what business has a believer with an unbeliever? What agreement hath the Temple of God with idols?"* In Jesus sayings the dualistic tendency is weaker. Instead of a contrast between God and Belial, there is here only the contrast between God and wealth. Through the Gospels, the Essenes' positive evaluation of poverty and the simple life and their essentially negative attitude towards wealth, influenced Christianity and became part of its social ideals.

Jesus not only refused to accept the Essene sectarian community of wealth, but he expressed opposition to their economic separatism. The Essene *"sons of light"*, restricted their economic ties with the environment to a minimum. *" No one must be united to him in his possessions and his poverty lest he loads upon him guilty sin but he should keep far away from him in everything. No one of the men of the community must either eat or drink anything of their property or accept anything whatsoever from them without paying for it. For all these are not reckoned within his covenant, they and everything they have must be excluded. The man of holiness must not lean on any works of nothingness, for nothingness of all who do not care for his covenant, for those who spurn his word he will destroy from the earth, for all their doings are pollution before him and impurity clings to all their property."* (Manual of Discipline V 13-20).

As we see therefore the social doctrines of Jesus was influenced of course by the Pharisees as well. Yet Jesus in his doctrine of love naturally opposed the economic Essene tradition. He said: *"The sons of this world are wiser than in their generation than the sons of light and I tell you, make for yourself friends from the mammon of the unrighteous."* (Luke 16:8-9) The wealth of the unrighteous is equivalent in the language of the sons of light from the Qumran to the wealth of the unrighteous of the non-Essenic communities. Thus, Jesus shared the Essenes positive attitude towards poverty and their suspicion of wealth, but because of his precept of unrestricted love, he opposed their economic attitude and did not accept their economic communism. But in subsequent development of Christian society in the middle ages, the concept of a separate community became part of the early church tradition with the establishment of their various religious orders. Thus, we see the late influence, which the Qumran community had on the development in the early church.

3)   The Orchard Redemption through Love

Traditionally, before the Jew observed Passover, he or she contributed to NAOT HITIM or *"the money for wheat."* Naot Hitim provided money for the needy. Also called KIMHA D'PESHA or *"the flour for Passover,"* this fund was established to reveal the compassion inherent in Mosaic law. But why was there a fund for Passover and not for Sukkot and Shavuot? Are there not just as many needy people around during these other two important festival times? Why only during Passover would we open the door at our Seders and announce, *"all who are hungry come and eat?"* Why, indeed is the same invitation not extended during Sukkot and Shavuot?

According to tradition, the Temple was destroyed and the Jews lost their independence because of Sinat Hinam, *"causeless hatred."* Their redemption will come through Ahavah *"loving kindness."* We are all to help the needy on all festivals, but especially is this true during Passover, the account the Jews' own liberation from slavery. Passover recalls liberation from difficult and impoverished existence as slaves in Egypt. Helping to free others from the slavery of poverty and want indeed helps remind the Jew that this is God's intention carried out by redeemed and free children of the Most High. On this coming Passover and every Passover we celebrate, we can say that we are fulfilling the important liberation of our Soviet brothers and sisters, over 400,000 of which have been freed in only three years. Along with these, virtually the entire Ethiopian Jewish community has found a new home in Israel.

Today, our support is most like Maot Hitin. It is giving money for the best cause, liberation and sustenance. We are working to make redemption of our Jewish brothers and sisters possible. We are giving that others may live in freedom in the land promised to them by God to Father Abraham and his seed. We are giving so that all may live without fear of persecution or progrom. Our fellow Jews are joined in the universal hope of life and freedom. That is what it means to fulfill this obligation. When we sit down at the Passover table let it be with the knowledge that we have done our part to make it so.

Chapter Six
Jewish and Christian Traditions
of Charity: Comparative Study

(1.0) **Introduction**

This chapter has for its object a systematic presentation of the Jewish and Christian traditions of charity, comparing the practices, which they have in common, and those which distinguish them. The purpose is not only to record factual data, but also to understand the nature and spirit of each religious tradition. This understanding can come only from examining the theoretical principles underlying the charitable system of each, as well as in the expression of these principles in the social and religious life of the Church and the Jewish community.

The early Christian Church was an offspring of the Jewish community. It carried into practice on the one hand, many of the Jewish conceptions of charity, which it adopted from its association with Jewish life; on the other hand, it acquired various traits and ideas from the Greco-Roman civilization, which made it foreign to the Jewish Weltanschauung. The present work is designed to trace this growth and development to the first three centuries of the Common Era, showing those characteristics, which made it similar to Jewish customs of benevolence, and those peculiarly Christian. This task will be limited to six comparative aspects:
(1) financial aid;
  (2) administration;
    (3) sensibilities;
      (4) impostors;
        (5) priorities, and
          (6)theological attitude.

First, we shall present the system and practice of charity in both the Christian and Jewish traditions in these six classifications. **Secondly**, we shall compare them, pointing out the features which parallel each other and which distinguish them.

In the field of the comparative study of the Christian and Jewish traditions of charity, almost nothing has been written, so far as the author can surmise. In consideration of the lack of secondary material, this essay relies entirely on the original sources. Our primary source is the Anti-Nicean literature of the Church Fathers, while the Jewish source is the Babylonian Talmud and Aggadic Midrashim.

In dealing with the problem of the comparative study of Christianity and Jewish charity, this short essay cannot make any claim to completeness, but it is hoped by the writer that further and more intensive research will be done in the future, as there is need for this kind of literature.

It is more than a pleasure to express my deep gratitude to the able guidance of my inspiring director, Dr. Abraham Cronbach, Professor of Jewish Social Studies at the Hebrew Union College. I am also indebted to Father John Dohenny, O.S.C. Professor of Church Law of the University of Notre Dame.

1a).Financial Aid in the Church

In the early beginning of Christian life there was no systematic collection of funds for the support of the poor. The opinion expressed by the Church Father Justin was typical of the early that was given except to provide for the most basic needs. Their attitude in giving was simply: *"Give to everyone that asketh of thee."*

However, when the Christian began to organize themselves into regular communities with Church life as the center of its religious existence, the collection of funds for the relief of the poor played a very prominent role in the life of the Church. Membership in the Church depended upon the individual's contribution of gifts to the life of the Church, which was one of the means by which the individual identified himself as a member of Church activities. The gifts which the individual Christian gave fell into two categories:

(1) gifts for the legal support of Church life;

(2) gifts for the public worship of God.

Every month the member of a Christian Church sent his contribution to the church chest. Tertullian designates there was no required sum demanded, but each was quite free to choose how much we will give. Tertullian states: *"On the monthly day, if he likes, each puts in a small donation, but only if it be his pleasure, and only if he be able for there is no compulsion; all is voluntary. These gifts are, as it were, piety's deposit fund."*

Similarly, Justin Martyr states that everyone of the Church should leave a voluntary contribution: *"They who are well to do and willing, give what each thinks fit; and what is collected is deposited with the president, who succors the orphans and widows, and those who are in want."*

However, we find that the Apostolic Constitutions designates it as "Corban". The apostolic Constitutions regard it the duty of every Christian to put something into the "Corban". *"If thou art not able to cast anything considerable into the Corban, yet at least bestow upon the strangers one, two or five mites."*

Besides these voluntary contributions made to the church chest the worshipers brought gifts of natural produce, called obligations, in connections with the celebration of the Lord's Supper. As it is recorded in Acts of the early community of Christian life, each one brought an obligation collected for an evening meal partaken of in common. For Acts states: *"They were preserving in the doctrine of the Apostles, and in the communication of the breaking of the bread and in prayers. And continued daily with one accord in the Temple, and breaking bread from house to house, they took their meat with gladness and simplicity of heart."*

The evening meal was known as the Agape, the love feast in which every member of the Church contributed according to his ability. The natural products were brought by the members of the Church and were collected by the deacons. Those ritual elements needed for the Holy Supper were placed upon the altar, while the rest of the produce was used for the support of the Church officers and the relief of the poor. Over these gifts a prayer of thanksgiving was recited: *"Let us pray for those that bear fruit in the holy church, and give alms to the needy."* After this prayer of thanksgiving, there followed the prayer of consecration and the bishop, presbyters, deacons, etc. partake of the holy bread and wine and distribute it to the people. The Apostolic Constitutions describe the ceremony in this manner: *"And let the bishop give the oblation, saying the body of Christ; and let him that receiveth say, Amen. And let the deacon take the cup; and when he gives it say, the Blood of Christ, the cup of life; and let him that drinketh say, Amen. And let the thirty-third Psalm be said, while all the rest partaking; and when all, both men and women, have partaken, let the deacons carry what remains into the vestry."*

From this description we may infer that the obligations offered, by no means consisted merely of the bread and wine for the Lord's Supper, but of natural products of all kinds. For, after everyone had partaken of the bread and wine, the deacons carry off the other products to the vestry room of the Church, where they were distributed for the support of the Church officers and the relief of the poor. These obligations, then, formed the chief financial means for the relief of the poor.

Even after the celebration of the Lord's Supper was separated from the Agape, and transferred to the morning service, these love feasts of the whole Church continued to be practiced as each contributed according to his means. Tertullian explains the purpose of the feast was not one of extravagant display of foods, but a dignified manner of helping the poor of the Church, and thus making them feel a part of Church life. For Tertullian lashes out against the heathen whose banquets are vain and licentious: *"with the good things of the beast, we benefit the needy. Not as is it with you, do parasites aspire to the glory of satisfying their licentious propensities, selling themselves for a belly-feast to all disgraceful treatment."* But he emphasizes that Christians have the love feast because the consideration of the poor is highly esteemed by God. Then Tertullian presents a description of the meal which, though somewhat idealized, still gives us an insight as to the nature of the feast: *"As it is an act of religious service, it permits no violence or immodesty. The participants, before reclining, taste first of prayer to God. As much is eaten as satisfies the cravings of hunger; as much is drunk as befits the chaste. They say it is enough as those who remember that even during the night they have to worship God; they talk as those who know that the Lord is one of their auditors. After manual absolution, and the bringing in of lights, each is asked to stand forth and sing, as he can, a hymn to God, either one from the holy Scriptures or one of his own composing - a proof of the measure of our drinking. As the feast commenced with prayer, so with prayer it is closed. We go from it, not like troops of mischief-doers, nor bands of vagabonds, nor to break our into licentious acts, but to have as much care of our modesty and chastity as if we had been school of virtue rather than a banquet."*

However, the spirit of the Agape must have degenerated to a very low degree as we later find that Tertullian speaks out very bitterly against it. Of it he says derisively, *"with you 'love' shows its fervor in saucepans, 'faith' its warmth in kitchen, 'hope' its anchorage in waiters."* Similarly, Clement of Alexandria speaks with vitriolic language against the love feasts in which they dare to apply the name Agape to pitiful suppers, redolent of savor and sauces. The Agape has ceased to be a common meal for the whole Church, but has become a meal for the poor prepared by any benevolent member and only the poor are invited. In the Apostolic Constitutions we discovered that at these meals aged woman were invited by the deacons who were actually in need of assistance.

Another means of supplying the Church funds for the relief of the poor were private obligations, which were brought in honor of the dead. The Apostolic Constitution alms were offered in memory of the deceased, which were taken from his property as a kind of memorial. Tertullian prescribes for newly married couples the following program: *"The sick is visited, the indigent relieved, with freedom. Alms (are given) without (damage of ensuing) torment."*

If the ordinary means of offering oblation did not suffice in the relief of the poor, or if some special emergency arose, these were obtained by a special collection. The Apostolic Constitutions instruct the bishop to make special collections if there is a definite need that has to be met: *"If a gift (oblations) be wanting, inform the brethren, and make a collection from them, and then minister to the orphans and widows in righteousness."* From a letter Cyprian wrote, we learn the particulars of such a collection. It happened that many Christians were made prisoners of war in Numidia and the bishops of that country needed help to ransom their brethren from captivity. Hence, they applied for help to Cyprian, who appointed officers to make a collection from both laity and clerics. Cyprian collected one hundred thousand sentences and submitted a list of those givers who contributed to the fund. He presented the money to the bishops, and specifically requested the bishops to offer up prayers for those who gave so willingly in the rescue of their brethren.

Besides the collections, made for special occasions certain, wealthy converts of the Church who joined turned over their wealth over to her treasure. When Cyprian was converted he sold his lands and gardens so that the funds might go to the Church in their support of the indigents. But this type of fund did not furnish the main supply of resources since the great body of the Christians still belonged to the lower economic strata. By far, the greater part was given, not by persons of property, but was on the contrary, the result of the small gifts of people of low condition who, as the Apostolical Constitution state, gave of their substance. In the writings of Hermas, the shepherd teaches his flock how to fast. He instructs them to abstain from drink and food, and devote this money for the help and support of the poor and widow. He states: *"And having reckoned up the price of the dishes you intended to have eaten, you will give it to a widow, or to some person in want, and thus you will exhibit humility of mind so that he who has received benefit from your humility may fill his own soul and pray for you to the Lord. If you observe fasting, as I have commanded, your sacrifice will be acceptable to God and this fasting will be written down and the service thus performed is noble, and sacred, and acceptable to God."* Similarly the Apostolic Constitutions also state the same idea: *"If anyone has not let him fast a day, and set apart that, and order it for the saints. But if anyone has superfluities let him minister more to them according to the proportion of his ability."* However, it was not the individual alone who employed this means of gaining funds, for the Apostolical Constitution prescribed that the bishop call a fast for the whole Church in order to apply what was thus saved to the wants of the needy.

The early Christians were quite conscious of the fact that they, like the Israelites, were obliged to bring their first fruits to the altar. For Irenaeus states: *"We are bound, therefore, to offer God the first fruits of His creation, Moses also says, so that man, being accounted as grateful, by those things in which he has shown his gratitude, may receive that honor which flows from Him."* However, Irenaeus maintains the New Testament to be advanced over the Old Testament since the former contains no external command, such as the demands that the Israelites gave by legal prescription. Yet, the very opposite opinion is held by Cyprian who bitterly complains that Christians actually gave less than one tenth of their earnings to the Church fund in the support of the poor. He reminds his fellow Christians that the primitive Church sold their possessions and gave the revenue for the maintenance of the needy. He bemoans the fact that in his time, less than one tenth is given to the charity fund of the Church. Although Cyprian does not make specific mention that giving one-tenth is the law of the Church, there is a ring in his words indicating that Cyprian was well inclined to make it a law. However, we discover that later the Old Testament commands about bringing the first fruits and one-tenth of the produce actually became a canon the Church. In the canons attributed to Hippolytus, the command specifically states that the faithful must bring the first-fruits of the barn floor and the wine press, of oil, honey, milk and wool, which are to be brought to the bishop who then pronounces a blessing upon them that they may serve for the care of the poor. Also, in the Apostolic Constitution there is a law which expressly declares Christians, on the ground of the old Testament law, be bound to give first-fruits and tithes:

"Wherefore you ought to love the bishop as your father, and fear him as your king, and honor him as your lord bringing to him your fruits and the works of your hands, for a blessing upon you, giving to him your first-fruits, and your tithes, and your oblations, and your gifts, as to the priest of God; the first fruits of your wheat, and wine, and oil, and autumnal fruits, and wool, and all things which the Lord God gives thee, and thy offering shall be accepted as a savor of a sweet smell to the Lord thy God; and the Lord will bless the works of thy hands, and will multiply the good things of the land." The law goes on further to state that although the sacrificing of animals for sin-offerings and burnt offerings are no longer binding upon the Christians, nevertheless, the Christian is still duty bound by the old law to bring his first fruits of other things, *"shalt thou give to the priests; but those of silver and of garments, and of all sort of possessions, to the orphan and to the widow, thou shalt give the tenth of thy increase to the orphan and to the widow and to the poor, and to the stranger."* This is an excellent illustration of how the gifts to the poor and the gifts to the priests merged into one another, showing the needs of the clergy and poor were considered as one and the same thing.

2a) Administration in the Church

As the collection of funds through the means of oblations was in the hands of the Church so, likewise, the administration of these funds was entirely in the hands of the officers of the Church. The relief of the poor, like the entire administration of Church affairs, was more and more concentrated in the person of the bishop. From the Epistles of Cyprian we perceive that the bishop exclusively administered the means for the poor, and that the deacons merely occupied a position of service, inquiring by order into the circumstances of the poor. However, the final decision was made only by the consent of the bishop. Only in the time of persecution when Cyprian was obliged to retire from Carthage for a period, did he divide the existing resources among the deacons and commission them to deal with them according to their judgment in alleviating the affliction and distress of the poor. Yet, Cyprian did not hereby give up this branch of charity work. The Apostolic Constitutions compare the bishop to a father and the deacons to sons: *"For as Christ does nothing without his Father, so neither does the deacon do anything without his bishop and as the Son without his Father is nothing, so is the deacon subject to his bishop; and as the Son is the messenger and prophet of the Father, so is the deacon the messenger and prophet of his bishop."* Thus, a deacon can give nothing to a poor person without the previous knowledge of his bishop. By doing otherwise, he would bring slander upon his bishop and disgrace the office of the bishop. Only the bishop is responsible to God for the management of the relief of the poor. Therefore, Apostolic Constitutions expressly enjoin a sacred duty upon the bishop to be extremely faithful and conscientious in the relief of the poor, giving them this command: *"O bishops, be solicitous about their maintenance (the poor), being in nothing wanting to them: exhibiting to the orphans the care of parents; to the widows the care of husbands; to those of suitable age, marriage; to the artificer, work; to the unable, commiseration; to the strangers, a house; to the hungry, food; to the naked, clothing; to the sick, visitation; to the prisoners, assistance."*

In the Epistles of Polycarp we discover that the presbyters who were ordained by the bishop and were of higher order than the deacons, also had besides their other duties, a specific duty towards the Church as regards the relief of the poor. Their main duty, as designated by the Polycarp, was the special care of the widows and orphans.

However, the real work of caring for the poor fell into the hands of the deacons. They were to be the eyes and ears of the bishop, through which he was to learn what was going on in the Church and who was in need of assistance. The deacons had the main task of collecting funds for the poor on behalf of the bishop and distributing these funds, according to the decisions of the bishop. Above all, they had to investigate strictly and in detail the circumstances of the poor. They went about from home to home, and whenever they found cases of distress, they immediately notified the bishop of them that he might make the necessary arrangements. But the Apostolic Constitutions specifically warns the deacon not to make any decisions on his own: *"For he gives up anyone as to a person in distress without the bishop and he accuses him as careless of the distressed, but he that casts reproach on his bishop, either by word or deed, opposes God by not harkening to what He says."*

However, the deacon is allowed a certain amount of freedom to dispose of small affairs without overburdening the bishop with too many intricate details. The Apostolical Constitutions impose this command upon the deacon: *"Let him order such things as he is able by himself, receiving power from the bishop, as the Lord did from his Father, the power of creation and of providence; the weighty matters let the bishop judge; but let the deacon be the bishop's ear, and eye, and mouth, and heart, and soul, that the bishop may not be distracted with many cares, but with such only as are more considerable, as Jethro did appoint for Moses, and his counsel was received."* The services of the deacon are as follows: *"to go about as the eyes of the inquiring into the doings of each member, ascertaining who is about to sin; to learn who are suffering under bodily disease and obtain help; to visit all those who stand in need of visitation and tell the bishop all those that are in affliction."* Thus, the deacon was a kind of patron of the poor constantly looking after their welfare. From Eusebius "Ecclesiastical History" we learn that there were seven deacons for each church. Besides the male deaconate, which rendered help to the male indigents, there was also a female deaconate who ministered to the needs of Christian women. In the first centuries they were known as widows. In the homilies of Clement on the institution of widows, widows constitute a regular part of the offices of the church, and as such being at the same time maintained by the church. They are at the head of the women in the church and impart instructions of church doctrine to the women and children. These women were older widows who had resolved never to remarry and were chosen for their work on account of their exemplary Christian life. Since the widows are always mentioned in connection with orphans, it is very natural that the care of the orphans was entrusted to the hands of these widows. In the Shepherd of Hermas, Grapte, a noted widow, is commissioned to care and instruct widows and the orphans.

Later, however, the institution of the widows was supplanted by the institutions of the deaconess. According to the Apostolical Constitutions the deaconess belonged to the clergy and received a special ordination with the rank of a sub-deacon.

Besides having a part in the church offices, the deaconess was also active in the care of the poor. They occupy, with respect to the female portion of the congregation, exactly the same position that the deacon does with respect to the male. The bishop could not send a deacon to visit the women, because of unbelievers, lest, as the Apostolic Constitutions say, evil reports should arise. That the administration of alms was the function of the deaconess is indicated by the mention of the quarrels between the widow who receives alms and the deaconess who grants alms. Also, when a woman desired to go to the bishop, she should do so only under the escort of a deaconess for the sake of decorum. The entire ministrations of the deaconate, so far as they relate to women are very expressly transferred to the deaconess. After describing the qualities of a deacon, it is said: *"And let the deaconess be diligent in taking care of the women; let everyone know his proper place, discharge it diligently with one consent, with one mind, as knowing the reward of their ministration; but let them not be ashamed to minister to those that are in want....as even our Lord Jesus Christ came not to be ministered unto, but to minister and to give his life a ransom for many. So therefore ought they be obliged to lay down their life for a brother."*

This office of the deaconate made it possible for the bishop to practice individual care of the poor, even to the smallest details. The services of the deacons and deaconess furnished him, on the one hand, with information of all the distress existing in the church, and on the other, gave the means of affording to everyone who was sick or poor, the just means of assistance. On the one hand, there was strict centralization, on the other hand , the utmost individualization...these were distinct features of Catholic charity.

3a) Sensibilities in the Church

As regards the sensibilities of the poor, the bishops are commanded to minister with great love and care. Their duty is to see that none who are in distress suffer from the lack of what is needed. They are to supply to orphans the care of parents, to widows that of husbands, to arrange marriage for those ready for marriage, to procure work for those out of work, to show compassion to those incapable of work, to provide a shelter for strangers, food for the hungry, drink for the thirsty, visits for the sick and help for the prisoners. The poor were to be highly esteemed and honored. It was to be no shame for them to receive alms. To the contrary, they were considered as the altar of God upon which the church lays its gifts; and if they sought to repay these gifts bestowed upon them, they do so by devout prayers and faithful intercessions for their benefactors.

While the deacons were to deal with the indigents in a very tender and sympathetic fashion, it was especially incumbent upon the poor that they should be contented, humble and devoted to God. It was impressed upon them with the utmost confidence that they had no right to support, but that it was love that offered it to them. They were always to regard what they receive as the gift of God who bestows it upon them by means of his faithful servant. *"Let the rich man provide for the wants of the poor, and let the poor man bless God because He hath given him one by whom his need may be supplied,"* as it is said in the Epistle of Clement. Thus, love was the motive of giving and a spirit of thankfulness was the sentiment of the recipient.

Although everyone who was in want received the assistance he needed, every effort was made to render the poor capable of work and to put them in a condition to earn their own livelihood. They were directed where to find work and were furnished with tools. Where there were still connections or relatives, the aid of these was first requested; they were not to cause the church any unnecessary burden with those whom it was their own first duty to help.

The church fathers recognized the position of the widow as one of honor and dignity. In order to alleviate the troubles of widows, the Apostolic Constitutions encouraged them to join the Order of Widows supported by the bishop. These widows are to be very grave and obedient to their superiors, the bishop and the deaconess. When the widows have been clothed by anyone or have received money, food, drink or shoes, they offer up this prayer upon seeing their sister widow who has received relief: *"Thou are blessed. O God, who hast refreshed my fellow widow. Bless, O Lord, and glorify him that has bestowed these things upon her, and let his good work ascend in truth to Thee, and remember him for good in the day of his visitations. And, as for my bishop who has ordered such seasonable alms to be bestowed on my fellow-widow, who was naked, do Thou increase his crown of rejoicing in the day of the revelation of Thy visitation."* They are not expected to complain about their lot but rather to accept it graciously. The Apostolic Constitutions warn against those widows who murmur against their deaconess: *"Those widows who will not live according to the command of God, are solicitous and inquisitive. What deaconess it is that gives the charity, and what widow receives it...she murmurs at the deaconess who distributed the charity? Why, therefore, hast thou preferred her before me?" She says these things foolishly not understanding that this does not depend on the will of man but the appointment of God."* Thus, the widows had many quarrels with the deaconess and the distribution of charity did not always meet with their favor.

Orphans, as well as widows, were also under the special guardianship of the bishop. He was to have brought them up at the expense of the church, and to take care that the girls be given to Christian husbands, when of marriageable age. Also, the orphan boys were to be taught some art and handicraft, and were then to be provided with tools and placed in a condition to earn their own living so that they might no longer be a burden to the church. Thus, the ideal kind of charity was that which ultimately led to self-support and encouraged the recipient by means of these gifts to earn a livelihood of his own.

4a) Impostors in the Church

The problem of impostors was dealt with in a very harsh and severe manner by the church fathers. They had no tolerance for those who received charity under false pretenses. The end of an impostor was utter damnation on the day of judgment as Isaiah 1:7 is interpreted: "Woe to those that have and receive in hypocrisy; or who are able to support themselves, yet will receive of others; for both of them shall give an account to the Lord God in the day of judgment. A person who could really work, and yet receives alms, robs the poor of his bread and the Lord will surely punish him."

However, to avoid the spread of impostors in the church, the deacons were obliged to make a very careful investigation into the needs of everyone who wanted assistance from the church. If the deacon found there was actual need of help he reported the matter to his bishop. When this had been done, they received the necessary aid. To this class belonged those who could no longer earn a livelihood or who, by joining the church, had lost their means of support because they had followed a trade or business, which the church did not permit. Yet it was strictly maintained that everyone should labor to the extent of his ability. Their point of view was mainly this: *"If anyone will not work, neither let him eat."* In the Didache it is ordained that no Christian wayfarer is to be maintained by any church for more than two or three days. Accordingly, the church had the prerogative of getting rid of such brethren. Yet, work was a vital duty: *"If any brother had a trade, let him follow that trade and earn the bread he eats. If he had no trade, exercise your discretion in arranging for him to live among you as a Christian, but not in idleness. If he will not do this, he is trafficking with Christ; beware of that man."* From this we can see that a Christian could demand work from the church, and that the church had by necessity of it's teaching, to furnish him with work. However, to those who had been obliged to relinquish their business, some other occupation was assigned, whenever possible, and they were not permitted to decline this, even if it was inferior to their former occupation. If they were unwilling to work, they received no aid. Conversion to the church was not to be made by idlers and impostors a source of worldly pleasure.

The church fathers not only condemned the impostors for receiving charity without want, but also were equally adamant against those who gave charity and oblations out of unjust gain and unrighteous wealth. The bishop is specifically warned not to receive the gifts of sinful persons: *"Now the bishop ought to know whose oblation he ought to receive, and whose he ought not. For he is to avoid corrupt deals and not receive their gifts."* Thus, the bishop could only take gifts given by Christians of a good conscience and such as led pure Christian lives. Heretics and excommunicated persons could bring no oblation. The Apostolic Constitution states: *"It is better to perish than to receive gifts from the enemies of God."* If, however such gifts are received unwittingly and unintentionally, they should be returned immediately so that the church might not suffer disgrace thereby.

5a) Priorities for Receiving Aid in the Church

Wherever there is mention by the early Christian writers of poor persons who require support, widows and orphans are invariably mentioned first and they seem to have priority over any other indigent. *"We learn from an admonition by Hermas in his writing 'Commandment' of the order of precedence and priority in lending support to the poor;*
(1) helping the widow,
(2) looking after orphans and the needy,

(3) rescuing the servants of God from necessities, being hospitable, practicing righteousness, being long-suffering." From this statement we can derive a system of priority in Catholic charity.

Besides the widows and orphans who took precedence in receiving charity funds, the sick were the next in line to obtain help from the Church's charitable gifts. It was the duty of the bishop to look after the needs of the sick. The deacons were also obliged to learn of those with bodily disease and bring it to the attention of the multitude that the needs of the sick be supplied.

In the early church there were no hospitals. The sick were attended in their own homes. The bishops, the presbyters and deacons made special calls on them there. The Canon of Hippolytus states: *"Of the bishop's visitation of the sick - if an infirm man had prayed to the church and has a house, he should go to him."*

The next mentioned in the list of priorities, as given by Hermes, was *"rescuing the servants of God from necessities."* Many Christians were imprisoned because of the debt or because of the practice of their faith. Both of these classes had to be reached through means of charity funds. These Apostolic Constitutions most impressively lay down the sacred duty of the members of the Church in regard to their attitudes toward prisoners: *"If any Christian, on account of the name of Christ, and in regard to their attitudes toward prisoners; and if any Christian, on account of the name of Christ, and the love and faith toward God, be condemned by the ungodly to the games, to the beasts, or to the mines, do not ye overlook him, but send him from your labor and your very sweat for his sustenance, and for a reward to the soldiers, that he may be eased and taken care of; that, as far as lies in your power, your blessed brother may not be afflicted; for he that is condemned for the name of the Lord God is a holy martyr, a brother of the Lord, the son of the Highest, a receptacle of the Holy Spirit, by whom everyone of the faithful has received the illumination of the glory of the holy gospel, being vouchsafed the incorruptible crown, and the testimony of Christ's sufferings, and the fellowship of His blood, to be made conformable to the death of Christ for the adoration of children. For this cause, do ye, all ye of the faithful by your bishop minister to the saints of your substance of your labor. But, if anyone has not, let him fast a day and set apart that and order it for the saints. But if anyone has superfluities, let him minister more to them according to the proportion of his ability. But if he can possibly sell all his livelihood and redeem them out of prison, he will be blessed and a friend of Christ. For if he, whoever gives his goods to the poor, is perfect, how much more will he be perfect who devotes all for the martyrs. "* Thus, redeeming a prisoner was highly rated by the church and was likened to a very saintly deed. Even when Christians were sentenced to the mines for punishment, they were still looked after while there. Their names were carefully noted; attempts were made for their release, and the Apostolic Constitutions speak of Christian brethren who were sent to ease the lot of the prisoners and hearten them.

However, the most important thing was not merely to alleviate the lot of prisoners, but to try and ransom them from prison. Ransoming captives was thus regarded as work especially noble and well pleasing to God a symbol of having a true imitation of Christ-like qualities. Yet, this was not carried on by the church directly, but through the generosity of certain individuals.

6a) Theological Attitudes in the Church

The central aim of Catholic charity in the first three centuries was not the healing of social wrong, nor the endeavor to remove poverty, but to awaken the spirit of love and charity as taught and lived by Christ. Jesus was, for the Christians, the highest incentive and directive of Catholic charity. *"For I was hungered and ye gave me meat; I was thirsty and ye gave me drink; I was sick, and ye visited me; I was in prison and ye came unto me...in as much as ye have done it unto one of the least of these, my brethren, ye have done it unto me."* The supreme ideal of Christian charity is ministering charity unto the poor as a practical expression of love to the Savior. Thus, the true way to love the Christ was by emulating his ideals and teachings.

Cyprian states: *"How much more could He (Christ) stimulate the works of our righteousness and mercy, than by saying that whatever is given to the needy and the poor is given to Himself, and by saying that He is aggrieved unless the needy and poor be supplied?"* The Christian is moved to give charity, not of the needs of his brother, but through his contemplation of the Christ. Whosoever despises his brother and refuses to give charity actually despises and reproves his Lord, who is identified with the poor and lowly. If a Christian gives charity, he is sure to receive a heavenly reward, and as Cyprian states: *"Let us give to Christ earthly garments, that we may receive heavenly rainment; let us give food and drink of this work that we may come with Abraham, Isaac and Jacob to the heavenly banquet; that we may not reap little, let us sow abundantly; let us, while there is time, take thought for our security and eternal salvation."* Thus, by doing works of charity one is assured of eternal life, and need have no fear for his redemption and salvation in the world to come. The best way to achieve immortal life is through the means of alms giving. By this one lends to God so that when one gives alms to the least, he gives them to Christ.

By alms giving, Cyprian declares that man becomes a partner with God. Through the poor he gives to God his earthly gains and receives from Him a portion of the heavenly kingdom: *"Divide your returns with the Lord, your God; share your gains with Christ; make Christ a partner with you in your earthly possessions, that he also may make you a fellow-heir with Him in His heavenly kingdom."*

Not only does alms giving prepare one for everlasting life, it is also the means for the atonement of our sins. *"Blessed are we",* writes St. Clement of Rome, *"if we fulfill the commandments of God in harmony of love, that through love, our sins were forgiven."* In the Epistles of Barnabas we read the admonition: *"Remembering the Day of Judgment, day and night, and seek each day the company of the saints, working with your hand for the ransom of your sins."* In a unique symbol, Hermes presents the blessings brought by alms giving. He compares the rich to the poles to which the vines are fastened. The pole itself bears no fruits, but so helps the vine that it can bring forth fruit. Thus, if the rich man prays little, his prayer is powerless. But, if he helps the poor, they pray for him, and their prayer is fruitful. The reason that God gives the rich man his wealth is because of the prayers of the poor.

In pleading with his fellow-Christians to give alms liberally, Cyprian states the rewards which come from giving: ...*"a wholesome guard of our security, a protection of hope, a safeguard of faith, a peace without the risk of persecution, the true and greatest gift of God."*

By doing charity, Cyprian explains that we are actually doing God's work. The only way to become sons of God is *"to imitate by the heavenly law the equity of God, the Father."* For just as God gives equally and liberally to all of the human race, so man imitates God when he, likewise, gives of what he produces to those who are in need and shares his returns and fruits with his fellow man. This was the way of the first Christians of the Church:

145

"They sold houses and farms, and gladly and liberally presented to the Apostles the proceeds to be dispensed to the poor; selling and alienating their early estate, they transferred their lands either where they might receive the fruits of an eternal possession, and there prepared homes where they might begin an eternal habitation."

For Cyprian, alms giving becomes one of the formal means of receiving grace; indeed, the only one which remains to a Christian after baptism, since baptism takes away only the sins which preceded it. Baptism, according to Cyprian, would be of little avail if God had not given man the means of giving, cleansing him of the defilement of sin. *"Prayers and fasting are unfruitful unless they are accompanied by alms giving. It is alms which gives power to prayer."* Entreaties alone are of little force to obtain what they seek unless they be made sufficient by the addition of deeds and good works. The angel reveals and manifests and certifies that our petitions become efficacious by good works. Furthermore, alms giving is a certain guarantee that our life is saved from dangers. The only real manner of appeasing God is through the medium of alms giving.

Poverty is not looked upon by the Church Fathers as an evil; on the contrary, it is a means of coming near to God. Cyprian regards property as a burden, and the rich are in his eyes fools since they increase their burden by keeping their wealth instead of letting the poor derive help from their riches. He demands that those who have suffered persecution and are wealthy should give up their riches and become true children of God. To give away property is, in itself, a good work; voluntary poverty is a higher moral condition than the possession of wealth.

1b)   **Financial Aid in the Jewish Community**

The most important means of financial aid for the

system of Jewish relief was the "Kuppah", or charity box. In ancient times, the Mishnah relates that in the Temple there was a "chamber of secrets" into which the pious ones deposited their gifts secretly and the poor families received support from it in secrecy. The charity box in the Talmudic period came to be known by the name "KUPPAH Shel Zedakah", a charity chest of the community which provided the means for the relief of the poor. So important and essential was this charity box for a community that no disciple of the wise was permitted to reside there unless a charity chest be present.

Everyone in the community was expected to contribute to the Kuppah according to the measure of his ability. A three-month resident was required to contribute to the Kuppah; a six month resident was obligated to the clothing fund; and he who lives in a city nine months had to contribute to the burial fund. Each must give according to his financial ability and particularly in consideration of the need of the time.

The Levitic tithing system was commonly regarded by the rabbis as the normal criterion, which meant giving ten per cent of one's profit. The maximum amount that was allowed to be given was twenty per cent. The rule of giving, for charity as a whole was considered a substitute of the Temple Tax and to replace sacrifices. A gift to the poor was looked upon as a substitute of the shekel given to the Temple for atonement. Thus, the ancient Temple cults served as symbol for the institutionalization of charity.

Another means of obtaining funds for charity was money given in connection with the liturgy and ritual. It was the practice of R. Eleazer to give a coin to a poor man before beginning the daily prayers, quoting the psalmist: *"With charity shall I behold Thy face."* This was most likely practiced by many Jewish saints who felt compelled by the liturgy to render aid to the indigents.

Besides the money that was given in connection with the liturgy, financial aid was also extended by means of a loan which, as a matter of course, was never collected. This was done in order to spare the sensibilities of the needy.

Every community had its "Kuppah Shel Zedekah" containing the funds collected for the support of the indigent townsmen, who received money every Friday for the fourteen meals of the entire week. The out-of-town poor had access only to the Tamhuy. For transients, other arrangements were made to receive bread and lodging, if so desired. The collections for the Kuppah were made weekly, while the collections for the Tamhuy were made daily. This provided for the main sources of the food needs of the indigents and always the available means of providing immediate help. However, not everybody was eligible to obtain help from the Tamhuy. That was available only for the poorest of the poor. He who had food for one day may not take anything from the Tamhuy.

The minimum to be given to a poor man who is on his way from one place to another is a loaf, which costs a Pundion when four measures of wheat are sold for selah. If he stays overnight, he is given his requirements for the night - bed, pillow, oil, fish and vegetables.

In time of emergency, when there was great need, special provisions were made by wealthy individuals, to cope with the situation. We read in the "Antiquities" of Josephus that during a great famine in Palestine, in the first century, Queen Helena of Adiabene bought shiploads of wheat and figs to aid the starving, and her son, Izates, sent great sums of money to the "foremost men of Jerusalem for distribution among the people." From this we may infer that already, in the first century, there existed in Jerusalem a body of men whose main duty was to distribute charity among the needy and receive special donations from wealthy individuals, such as Queen Helena of Adiabene.

At different times, there were special Rabbinic committees, who traveled from community to community to collect funds and means for the support of the students of Torah. Beside the support of the students of Torah, there had to be special provisions made for orphans, by seeing them married and launched in life for themselves, with furnished homes and dowries. There were also other provisions made for the redemption of captives, caring for the sick, and burying of the dead.

Another source of income for the charity fund was the generous donations made by wealthy persons. We read that Mar Ukba gave half of his wealth to charity before he passed away with this exclamation: *"The provisions are scanty and the road is long."* Also, Monobaz (a king who was converted from heathenism to Judaism) gave away all of his riches to the needy in time of drought.

2b)   Administration in the Jewish Community

In the Jewish community the matter of charity and relief for the poor was not merely the concern of the individual but the responsibility of the entire community, whose obligation was to care for those in need. Every community appointed collectors, men of excellent character and fine reputation. They were so deeply trusted that they did not have to render an account of the money entrusted to them for charitable purposes. The Kuppah was collected by two persons, the understanding being that any office, which has authority over the community, has to be filled by at least two people. However, three administrators were required for the distribution of charity, since they are regarded as a type of Beth Din which have to weigh and decide the claims of the indigents and make investigations concerning their actual need. This follows the analogy of monetary cases, since three men only possess judicial authority. Every Friday the collectors went about their rounds to the shops, collected money or other necessary things, and sought contributions from the rich. Many times this would naturally lead to violent quarrels with collectors whose position was not always enviable. The Gaggai had to be careful to avoid conflict nor overstep his bounds and become oppressive.

The distribution of the Kuppah was made on a Friday. On Friday, to provide food for the poor for the coming week, they were given fourteen meals. Clothing was also furnished to those who needed it. If a new resident, from another city, was out of funds, he could likewise receive aid from this collection.

The position of the Gabbai was not sincere. It entailed a great deal of responsibility and difficulty in distributing charity in an equitable fashion so as not to offend the delicate feelings of the indigents. R. Jose very clearly expresses this difficulty when he states: "May my lot be of those who collect charity but not of those who distribute it." Evidently, the job of distribution was one which required such skill and art that very few were actually qualified for the intricate task and most of them suffered such heartache from the position that it was not likely to be relished by many.

Since the distributors endured so many hardships, it is very understandable that many would decline the position. This is the very situation, which R. Jose had to deal with in his community. It seems that in the city of Kaphra, he had to face a deeply embarrassing situation when everyone he appointed to the office of Parnass, declined the position. In order to induce the members of his community to accept the office he had to praise the Parnassim as one of great merit and worthy of being counted the greatest of the generation. R. Haggai employed another technique. He would preach that the appointment is not human but divine, and thus, perhaps, in this manner he would be able to encourage the members of his community to accept the office in a more gracious manner.

There were a number of regulations to guide the Gabbaim to avoid suspicion, and misunderstanding and keep from casting shadows upon the character of these noble men. These rules were the following: The Gabbaim, when collecting for charity were not permitted to separate from each other, though one could collect near the city gate while the other collects at the shops near the gate, since they would be in sight of each other and each could check on possible acts of embezzlement on the part of the other.

If one of the collectors, while collecting, found money in the street, he was not permitted to put it into his own purse as the people might then say that he was misappropriating charity funds. Thus, he was required to put that which he found into the charity box. On coming home, he could take it out. If one of the collectors was being paid a debt in the street, he could not put the collected money collected from his debtor into his own pocket. Thus, in order to avoid suspicion he would put it into the charity box and remove it only after he has arrived home.

When the time would come that the collectors had money but no applicants, to whom it should be distributed, they needed to change the small coins into larger ones. However, the changing should be with other persons and not with the collector's own money. The reason being that people might say that they did not give full value to the exchange. The very same thing applied to the stewards of the soup kitchens who had food left over and no poor to give it to; they could sell it to others but never to themselves.

In counting out money collected for charity, the Gabbaim should not count the coins two at a time because people might allege that they were taking money. Therefore, the collector must count only one coin at a time. Still, they were implicitly trusted and not required to render an account of the money entrusted to them.

Besides the collectors for the Kuppah, there were also collectors for the Tamhuy who went to collect from house to house. In contradistinction to the Kuppah, the Tamhuy required three collectors to go about to receive the food stuffs since it had to be distributed as soon as it was received. While the Kuppah was distributed only to the poor of the town, the Tamhuy served for all comers.

The administrators made investigations into their applicants so as to avoid impostors. The rabbis questioned as to whether the applicants for food or clothing should be exempt from examination. R. Huma holds the opinion that one who is in need of clothing should be exempt from an investigation since his ragged appearance reduced him to a state of degradation. But Reb Judah is inclined to favor the exemption of the applicant for food who is actually suffering from a physical discomfiture. The position of the administrators of charity of the Jewish community had to face a difficult situation with regard to dealing with the poor and constantly had to contend with the censorship of the community leaders.

3b)   Sensibilities in the Jewish Community

In administering charity there was always present a deep regard for the sensibility of the poor. The rabbis were constantly aware that the poor must in no way be put to shame. We are told of an incident wherein a rabbi admonished a giver of charity with these words: *"It would be better that you did not give anything at all, rather than that you give it in such a way as to put the poor man to shame."* Everything was done to guard the feelings of the poor and to avoid all possible embarrassments. "Better a man throw himself into a fiery furnace than publicly put his neighbor to shame." The giver of charity in secret was extolled as being greater than Moses.

All possible secrecy was maintained in order not to offend the recipients of charity. Rabba would go to the extent of throwing his gift behind him, wrapped in a scarf, in order to make himself unknown to the recipients. If a man refused to accept charity because of hypersensitivity, the rabbis sought to spare his feelings by allowing him to take a gift form of a loan, which they did not try to collect. We read of a story of wealthy man who was reduced to poverty but, because of his former high status, refused to accept charitable aid: yet, R. Jannai induced him to accept a gift in the form of a loan, since he related to him that he had again become wealthy through the great fortune of a dead relative in a far-off land. Thus, the rabbis used wisdom and discretion to overcome embarrassing the poverty-stricken man seeking to loan money to the poor before they asked for it.

Besides helping the poor to a means of self-support, the rabbis were very conscious of the delicate modesty of womanhood. When an orphan girl and boy seek assistance, the girl is shown the first consideration because the dignity of woman does not permit her to go about begging. Furthermore, when the funds were available, the social position of the orphan girl was seriously considered and she was furnished with a dowry and other provisions, in accord with her dignity. Every attempt to administer aid wisely, and with a sense of dignity, was made in order that the morale of the dependent be lifted.

The rabbis were very considerate of the sensibilities of the poor in seeing that adequate provision was made for each person. The principle was that he who needs bread is granted bread; he who needs dough is given dough; he who is in need of grain is given grain. Every case had to be judged on its merits. Even the former aristocrat had to be given the type food to which he was accustomed in the past; the delicate individual was treated according to his standard. We have recorded a very beautiful account of this fact in the Talmud: *"Our Rabbis taught: it once happened that the people of Upper Galilee bought a pound of meat daily for a poor member of a good family. According to the various interpretations, it was a pound of fowl's meat or ordinary meat for a pound of money; or the place was a small village where there are no buyers and no consumers; thus, every day a beast had to be spoiled for his sake."*

Another story of Mar Ukba illustrates a certain humor in his consideration for the delicate feelings of the poor. Mar Ukba was accustomed to send four hundred zus to a poor person in his neighborhood. However, when he heard from his son that the poor man was of elegant taste, he doubled his gift. Similarly, the famous story of Hillel, the Elder, who not only provided an indigent with the very best of food and drink, but also gave him a horse to ride and a slave to run before him. Once Hillel found himself in the position where he could find no slave and he, himself, ran for three miles before the poor man. It happened once that R. Nehemiah failed to meet the refined needs of the indigent person, and because of this the poor man passed away.

The ideal personalities, especially noted for their consideration of the sensibilities of the poor, were Abraham and Job. Each had the four doors of his home open to the weary travelers so that regardless of what direction they might be going, the door of hospitality and kindness was open to them. It is also asserted that Abraham and Job erected public inns on the high roads, offering food and shelter to the poor wayfarer. In Babylon, Huna bar Hanilai followed this same tradition by maintaining an inn with its four doors open on four sides for all passers-by. In addition to this, sixty bakers were kept busy day and night supplying bread to all those in need of sustenance. According to an enactment made by Ezra, the housewife was required to rise early in the morning to bake bread so that there was sufficient bread in time for the poor. All of these traditions and practices of the Talmudic period indicated the deep concern the rabbis had for the sensibilities of the poor and the length to which they went in order to protect their welfare.

4b)   **Impostors in the Jewish Community**

The attitude of the rabbis toward impostors was neither strict nor harsh but one of sympathetic understanding and humane liberality. This is especially exemplified by many Rabbinic statements and stories in the Talmud. The story is told that R. Hanina had the habit of giving four zus to a poor man of his neighborhood. One day he sent his wife to deliver the money. She discovered the indigent discussing with another person whether to use a gold or silver cloth for dinner. In view of this incident, R. Eleazer made the following statement: *"Come, let us be grateful to the rogues (impostors) for were it not for them we would have been sinning every day for it is said in Scripture, 'and he cry unto the Lord against thee and it be sin unto thee.'"* Thus, one should be charitable to all persons, whether they are in need or not. The fact that impostors do exist is no reason for one to be less charitable since as R. Joshua B. Korha maintained: *"Any one who shuts his eye against charity is like one who worships idols."* Therefore, the rabbis held a humane point of view in dealing with all indigents; even if some were deceivers. They urged their people to be liberal at all times rather than to become stingy because of some impostors. If a man accepts charity without needing it, he will eventually be punished, for he will actually be in need of charity some day.

However, even those who gave liberally were very cautious to whom they gave. When R. Abba bound his money in a scarf before slinging it behind his back for the benefit of the poor, he would cautiously look to see if there were any impostors around. R. Abba held the opinion that being tricked into giving to the unworthy is actually punishment for sins committed: *"Jeremiah said to the Holy One, blessed be He, even at the time when they conquer their evil inclinations and seek to do charity before Thee, cause them to stumble through men who are not fitting recipients so that they should receive no reward for assisting them. But if a man really wants to give charity, and is of a pure character, God not only provides him with the means to give, but likewise assures him of fitting recipients who will ring him a true and lasting reward."*

The ultimate solution to the problem of impostors, according to the rabbis, did not lie in the fact of warning the givers, but seeking preventive means of saving the recipients of charity from falling into such a state. Therefore, they urged every manner of labor, even to the point of hiring oneself out to an uncongenial calling, rather than be in need of the help of one's fellow creatures. Nothing was looked upon as being too low and undignified.

The rabbis taught that one should endeavor to be frugal even in the observance of holidays and the Sabbath. Similarly, a control was placed upon the limit of being charitable. At Usaha it was ordained that not more than twenty per-cent of the benefactor's income be given to charity lest, by extravagant giving one might himself become a recipient.

Another preventive means imposed by the rabbis was the duty of every father to teach his son a trade. According to R. Judah - anyone who does not perform this obligation of teaching his son a trade is as if he were instructing his son in burglary. This was the practical maxim of the rabbis concerning teaching a craft: *"A man should always teach his son a cleanly craft and let him pray to Him to whom riches and possessions belong, for there is no craft wherein there is not both poverty and wealth, for neither poverty comes from one's craft, nor riches from one's craft, but all is according to one's merit."*

Although Maimonides held the opinion that the highest degree of benevolence was the making of a loan or gift which sought to reconstruct and restore life to its normal pattern of self-support, we do not find support for this idea in the Talmudic sources. The passages of Talmudic literature do speak of loans, business partnerships and other such means of financial help whose underlying motive seems to be the desire to avoid humiliating the feelings of the indigent.

5b)   Priorities for Receiving Aid in the Jewish Community

In the system of Jewish charity, redemption of captives merits priority over every other cause involving even that of the indigent, in as much as the captive is potentially exposed to the most dreadful treatment at the hands of his brutal captor. A very interesting discussion concerning this problem is related in the Gemara: *"Whence is it inferred that the redeeming of captives is the greatest death; such as for the sword; and such as for famine."* Concerning which, R. Johanan said: *"Each instance mentioned in this series is more tragic than the one preceding it. As, for instance, to be killed by the sword is severer than to die a natural death, for to be slain by the sword is to become disfigured. Still worse is famine, which is a slow and prolonging form of life, ebbing away, accompanied by continuous pangs of hunger, while the sword ends life speedily. But the fate of the captive may even be more horrible than the lot of any other victim because this form faces the potential danger of unimaginable tortures and death. Therefore, no precept equals in significance the one relating the redemption of captives."*

Thus, when funds have been collected for the purpose of building a synagogue, they can be used for the cause of redeeming captives. Moreover, though stones and beams have already been prepared for the building of the house of worship, these can also be sold for the purpose of freeing the captives. However, if the synagogue has already been built, it shall not be sold, but finished; and collections to be made from the congregation, for the work of redemption.

There is also a definite order of priority wherein sex has precedence in receiving charitable aid. Thus, when both men and women are in captivity, the woman must be released first because of the potential assailability of her honor. However, when both stand in danger of perdition, the man must be freed before the woman because he fills more precepts of the Torah than a woman. An orphaned girl is to be furnished with garments prior to an orphaned boy because her modesty is greater than his. A woman is to be given food sooner than a man since a man can go about and beg, which is beneath the dignity of a woman. Therefore, if an orphan-boy and an orphan-girl apply for grants to be betrothed, the girl shall be helped by the charity fund before the boy because the sensitiveness of a woman are greater.

If there be many captives and not enough funds to redeem them all, this order is recommended: *"A Kohen is preferred to a Levite; a Levite to an Israelite, and an Israelite to a bastard; a bastard to one of uncertain paternity; one of uncertainty paternity to a foundling; a foundling to a mamzer; a mamzer to nathin; and a nathin to a proselyte; a proselyte to a freed Canaanite slave."*

However, this rule applies only when all the applicants are of equal talents; *"but if the mamzer is a Talmud Hacham and the High Priest is an am-Haretz, the learned mamzer is preferred to the High Priest. A scholar takes precedence over a King of Israel because, if a scholar passes on, there is none to take his place, while any Israelite can replace a King."* Thus, we infer that learning determined also the preference in giving relief and that a scholar was sure of receiving preference when it came to giving charitable aid.

So deep was the love of learning and reverence for the scholar that the redemption of one's teacher was preferred, even over one's own father, the reason being that the teacher brings one into the world to come. However, the law stipulates that if the father is learned in Torah, he gets the first consideration.

However, as regards the priority of the ego in matters of charity, we are unable to locate a passage, which would definitely substantiate the ego as a candidate for priority in the receiving of alms.

6b)   **Theological Attitudes in the Jewish Community**

"What has God been doing since He created the world?" asked a Roman matron. *"The Holy One praised be He,"* answered R. Jose, *"constructs ladders whereby He elevates one person and lowers another, as it is said, 'He humbleth one and He lifteth up another."* From this Midrash we can gather a very interesting definition of God as the everlasting prime mover of the cosmic wheel of fortune, as the continuous enricher and improverisher of men. It is God alone who makes men either to ascend the ladder of monetary success or brings him down in utter poverty. Thus, every man who has attained wealth should feel an obligation to the poor, for tomorrow he has no knowledge of whether he, too, will find himself in the same position. The world was looked upon as the rotating wheel

of a well; the earthenware vessels attached to it ascend full
from below and descend empty from above. Similarly, the
rich may not find himself in the same condition tomorrow,
and so the poor man may not find himself in the same
straits. If a rich man is greedy and begrudges giving of his
wealth, he will find himself later in a state of chaos. God
offers to man a means of redemption - charity. Through the
giving of charity man obtains his redemption. As R. Judah
stated: *"Great is charity, in that it brings the redemption
nearer. Charity is an intermediary which brings Israel
closer to God, for through the works of charity and loving
kindness that Israel performs, there is promoted a feeling of
peace and understanding between God and Israel."*

But charity is a means of performing God's work
here on earth. When a poor man complains of his lot and is
helped by benefactors, they are actually helping to make
peace between God and the poor. By caring for them, we
become God's creditor, since: *"he that is gracious unto the
poor, lendeth unto the Lord." "If it had not been for a
written text,"* say the rabbis, *"the statement dared not have
been uttered; if the expression be permitted, it is usual for a
borrower to become the servant of the lender."*

By the maintenance of the poor, the doer of charity
benefits through the recipient. He places himself in a close
position to God and puts Him under obligation: *"Since this
man comes and snatches up the good deed, the Holy One,
blessed be He, says: 'I must pay him recompense.'"*

The story is told of Benjamin the Righteous, who
supported a widow and seven children from his own pocket
when the charity funds had been completely drained. It is
told the Almighty rewarded him with an extra twenty-two
years of life. So it is with every man who does charity; he
receives twenty-four blessings. Likewise, the doer of
charity is delivered from trouble and is assured long life and
prosperity; he is also saved from death, like the wood

chopper who bestowed bread upon an old person and thereby was saved from certain death when, without knowing it, he chopped the serpent who was lurking nearby, into pieces.

"*Give unto Him what is His,* " says the Mishnah, "*for thou and what thou art are His, for all things come from Thee, and of Thine own have we given Thee.*" Thus, what the poor man receives is not the rich man's contribution, but God's allotment. Charity then becomes a duty rather than an act of kindness, a kind of debtor's payment for what rightly and divinely belongs to him without even the need of offering thanks for what he receives.

In seeking to replace the Temple cult with its intricate system of atonement, the rabbis viewed charity as the true substitute for the ancient sacrifice with its expiatory function. Charity assumed the importance of a sacrament. "*He who bestows hospitality upon a student of the Torah is as if he had offered the daily burnt offerings. The coin to the needy is the Temple's "Shekel" - the food to the hungry is the Temple's offering. Therefore, every doer of charity is a priest, every table where the poor are fed is an altar, and every gift a sacrifice. Charity offers man the means of making atonement for his past sins. It is actually tantamount to performing all the religious Mitzvot enjoined in the Torah: Charity is equivalent to all the other religious precepts combined.*" Some rabbis went a step further in the theological merits of charity by saying that philanthropy is worth more than all of the sacrifices.

Charity is a great virtue because the poverty, which it relieves, is a greater evil. "*Nothing is harder to bear than poverty; for he who is crushed by poverty is like one to whom all the troubles of the world cling and upon whom all the curses of Deuteronomy have descended.*" Furthermore, the rabbis held the opinion that if all the troubles of the world were on one side, poverty would outweigh all of them. It is told of Job that when he was given a choice between poverty and the other forms of suffering, he selected the latter because poverty is worse than fifty plagues. He who is obliged to apply for charity to his fellow man is as if two judgments of fire and water were passed upon him. Not a single day in the life of the poor is good, including even the Sabbaths and festivals.

On the other hand, we discover that poverty, as such, was not regarded as exclusively evil. We find instances paradoxically enough, where poverty is praised as the very foundation of sympathy and the means of loving-kindness. For it is through poverty that the humaneness of man becomes possible and needful. It is the poor that offer the rich an opportunity to do kindness and to gain the world to come.

From this we can see that poverty was not entirely a curse, according to Rabbinic thought. Rabbi Akiba held the opinion that the poor exist in order to enable the better circumstanced to escape hell fire through their benevolences.

(1.1) Comparing the Catholic and Jewish Traditions of Charity

In our study comparing the early Catholic and Jewish traditions of charity of the first three centuries we have tried to parallel their practices and usages in six respects: (1) financial aid; (2) administrators; (3) sensibilities; (4) impostors; (5) priorities, and (6) theological attitudes. Generally we have noted that charity plays an integral part of each religious tradition. It formed a very vital role in the life of the Church and the Jewish community. It governed their thinking, molded their religious outlook, and formed the center and core of their religious beliefs and doctrines. The practices and institutions of charity in both religions reflect the spirit and structure of its whole. Those things, which make the religious traditions what they are, are definitely and explicitly expressed in their different practices and customs. These we shall note in the following order:

1c)   Comparison of Financial Aid

For both the Church Fathers and the Rabbis, charity was one of the chief means by which the individual identified himself with his respective religion. Membership in the Church was dependent upon a Christian's contribution of gifts to the life of the Church. The Jewish community, and likewise the Jew, identified himself with the life of the community by contributing to the Kuppah after three months of residence, and after six months to the Clothing Fund. Both had a special charity box into which contributions were made. The Kuppah was found in every Jewish community. Since the Christians called their charity box "Corban" (meaning sacrifices) they probably took over this practice from their Jewish brethren. The Church always considered itself the true heirs of the Temple and sought to institute those things in the Church which were formerly part of the ancient Temple. Collections for the "Kuppah" were made once a week while the collections for the "Corban" were made once a month. Both the Rabbis and the Church Fathers felt themselves bound to the Levitic system of tithing, and both prescribed the normal criterion for giving charity to be ten per cent of one's income. Charity for Judaism and Catholicism becomes a substitute for the ancient system of sacrifices and replaces the Temple offerings.

In the early church, bringing gifts and oblations to the poor was part of the ritual of the church. They brought these things in connection with the celebration of the Lord's Supper. The only Jewish parallel known is the practice of

R. Eleazer, who gave money to the poor before he began his daily prayers. Other than this example, charity was not brought to the synagogue in connection with the ritual while in the church it played a central role.

Besides the placing of money into the charity box, food played a central part, as regards both the early church and the Jewish community. According to the church fathers, the early Christians brought oblations of food and partook of a common meal in the evening, called the Agape. The Jewish practice was to collect victuals every day for the Tamhuy (charity bowl) and to distribute them daily to the hungry indigents who did not partake of a common meal, but were each provided with sufficient food for their subsistence. The difference between the two practices was that the Agape was deeply connected with the ritual and liturgy of the church while the Tamhuy was concerned with only meeting the practical needs of the poor.

There are direct parallels in the Catholic and Jewish sources which show that converts to the Church, and Synagogue made large contributions to the charitable funds. Upon the conversion of Cyperian to Catholicism and King Monobasz to Judaism, both gave almost all of their financial resources to the relief and help of indigents.

The giving to the poor in the form of a loan is a Jewish practice which has no parallel in Catholic sources. On the other hand, the Catholic practice of fasting in order to use such money for the help of the needy has, as far as we know, no equal in Jewish tradition. However, when a fast did take place in a Jewish community, the poor were not permitted to suffer as a result of such fast.

2c)   **Comparison of Administrations**
The Jewish community had no official ecclesiastical head in charge of the administration of charity, as did the early Roman church. The administration of charity in the

church was done according to strict monarchical form. The bishop was the absolute administrator of charity in his diocese and the final authority in all matters of administration. His assistant workers were the presbyters, deacons, sub-deacons and deaconess - all of whom were under his special jurisdiction. In striking contrast to this system, the administration of charity in the Jewish community moved along more democratic lines. First, the Gabbai were appointed by the community and were comparatively free to do their work without having to pay deference or obedience to any outside authority. Secondly, the collectors were laymen who did not have to be ordained to the office of the clergy, as was so rigidly observed in the Catholic system.

There are, however, many similarities between the Gabbai and the deacon. Both had the main duties of collecting and distributing charity; and both had a certain set of rules and regulations, which they were obligated to follow. The rules governing the deacon were very exacting. He had to be the ear and eye of his bishop and he could do nothing of his own volition - without the consent of a higher authority. The deacon was also required to carefully investigate every case. In comparison to this sort of discipline the Gabbai was relatively free to do what he considered best. He was not compelled to submit a list of applicants, but did make an investigation of indigents to see that there were no impostors present among them. The Gabbai was deeply trusted in his position and no investigation was ever made of his work nor did he have to render an account of the money, as was the case with the deacon. However, he had to put up with many complaints, which tended at times, to make his position somewhat unpleasant. However, the deacon and deaconess of the church had almost the same problem with which to contend. There were seven deacons for every church while the Jewish community had two collectors and three distributors.

3c)   **Comparison of Sensibilities**
        In dealing with the sensibilities of the poor, the church fathers and the rabbis were deeply attentive to the delicate feelings of their recipients. Both sought means to avoid any kind of embarrassment which might afflict the sensitive nature of the poor. The Jewish practice was that of secret giving while that of the Catholics was to develop a kind of giving which would bring honor and esteem to the poor and make them feel a sense of importance. The rabbis and the bishops sought to obtain that kind of charity, which would adequately and sufficiently meet the wants of the needy.
        The bishops tried to secure husbands for the widows and parents for the orphans so that they would no longer have to be dependent upon the church's fund for further aid, and the same is true of the Jewish community. The rabbis encouraged a gift in the form of a loan, which was never collected, seeking to lend money to the indigent even before he requested it.

4c)   **Comparison of Disposition of Impostors**
        The rabbis and the church fathers held opposite opinions concerning impostors. For the church nothing was so abhorrent as an impostor. He was to be utterly condemned on the Day of Judgment and receive his due punishment. The rabbis, on the contrary, were more liberally minded and various stories in the Talmud and Midrash indicate their humaneness and sense of humor as regards deceivers. Being inveigled into giving to impostors was an indication of being sinful. It was held that only the benefactor of a pure spirit could be assured that he was contributing to worthy recipients.

Although the rabbis and church fathers held opposite views in their attitude toward impostors, they were one in seeking to remedy the situation. Both advocated a program of work and labor and had only contempt for the idler. Although the church made provisions for those who were unable to work, the church was very strict in her discipline to see that everyone worked and had a trade. Idleness was never tolerated, and if there was no work to be found on the outside, the church itself provided work for the indigents. The same attitude can be found in the Talmud. The Rabbinic ideal man was the one who earned his own livelihood by the sweat of his labor. We do not find quite the same emphasis in the literature of the church fathers. There is also not the same practical approach and effective way of giving, as we find in Rabbinic literature.

5c)   **Comparison of Priorities**
        In the church as well as in the Jewish community there were definite gradations of giving charity and certain preferences were maintained. According to the church fathers the widows and orphans needed priority over any other class of indigents. In the system of Jewish charity it was the redemption of captives that was of first priority, but woman were nearly always given special consideration after captives and because of their need for modesty, were the first to receive aid.
        In the Catholic system the learned and the scholarly person received no special priority. In this system, it was the hierarchy, the ordained, who received the honor and consideration, while the learned received no special attention. The contrary was true in the Jewish community, where a learned mamzer had preference over a High Priest, who was Am Haretz.

6c) Comparison of Theological Attitudes

As the God of the Fathers was the ideal for the Jewish concept of charity, so was the Christ for the Catholic conception. In both systems charity was the means of knowing and performing God's will. For the Catholic, charity was a practical expression of the Christian's love of his Savior; for the Jew the doing of charity was becoming God's helper. Eternal salvation and a place in the heavenly realms was reserved for those who give alms. But more than this, charity actually became a sacrament in both religious systems. For the Catholic, alms giving is a formal way to receive the grace of Christ; for the Jew it is as if he had observed all the precepts of the Torah. For both, alms giving brings atonement and deliverance from death and sin.

Poverty in the Catholic system is generally regarded a supreme virtue while, according to the rabbis, it is a supreme ill. The rabbis are not all consistent regarding this point since there are some who extol poverty almost to the same degree, as do Catholics. There are instances in Rabbinic literature where poverty becomes a way for man to reach God through his help of the poor. This identical thought is found in the church fathers; poverty being the means of coming nearer unto the Christ.

Chapter Seven
Separation of the Church from the Synagogue

1)   **Some Conclusions**

Jewish roots within Christianity is an historical fact. It is also clear that Christianity constituted a new community, distinct from Judaism. Christianity is in the peculiar position of becoming a religion because of its Jewish roots. In a real sense, Christianity is obliged to be occupied with Judaism. Conversely, a Jew can live his Jewish religious life without having to wrestle with the problems of Christianity. Judaism did not come out of Christianity. Christianity came out of Judaism. From its very beginnings, Christianity understood itself more or less as an heir of Judaism in that truest expression. At the same time, it knew it had many common factors with Judaism, while often failing to acknowledge Judaism's fundamental contribution to what would become a new religious expression. What initially caused the split between the early Church and the Synagogue? Were there factors that led to two separate religions?

To deal with these issues we need to first review and examine several other examples. Throughout human history, new religions or religious communities have arisen from previous religious communities. For example the growth of Buddhism grew out of a prior Hinduism. The fact that a new religion grows out of an old religion has been a part of the process of human civilization.

We have to understand that Christian anti-Judaism was almost inevitable, given the social/political climate of the first several centuries of the Common Era. In another sense, the religious falling out that finalized the end of the first century can be understood as a sociological phenomena. The same dynamics that often govern family relations have their parallel in the conflict that characterized Jewish and Christian relations. In modern times, we have examples such as the Church of Jesus Christ of Latter Day Saints, whose members surely have their origins in Christianity. We may ask ourselves whether they represent a Christian sect or a new religion ? That question parallels the question of the relationship of Judaism and Christianity. It is the same question that forms around any group that evolves out of another group.

From such observations we may deduce that as the early Church grew out of the Synagogue it was bound to separate from its original community. From the beginning it was known both to Jews and Christians that they believed in the same God. Today, more than in centuries past, Jews and Christians are able to appreciate the common Jewish values which Christianity inherited from the Synagogue and then developed in its own special way.

Paul said that Jesus was born *"under the law"*, (Gal.:4) and that he became a servant of the circumcised to maintain the truth of God by making good his promises to the patriarchs (Rom.. 15:8). Today, scholars recognize that Jesus was a pious Jew, living as did other Jews, according to the Laws of Moses, as practiced in his day, and that he recommended this religious way of life to his disciples. It is also generally accepted that Jesus did not preach a new religion. His debates with the Pharisees were not to arouse anger or enmity, but to demonstrate his way of interpreting the Law using the common mode of discourse of his day. Nevertheless, his ministry had a revolutionary/radical impact on the world.

At the death of Paul, Christianity was still a Jewish sect. In the middle of the second century, it becomes a separate religion, busily engaged in preaching to Greeks and Romans and establishing its own antiquity, respectability and loyal followers.

It is a daunting task to decide on a date when the final separation took place. Several factors characterizing this moment can be considered. First, when the armies of Titus approached Jerusalem, Jewish Christians retired to Pella. About the same time, rabbinical leaders retired to Yavneh. The defense of Jerusalem was undertaken by political and not religious leaders. With the fall of the city, the two religious groups showed different effects. The rabbinical leaders, in some part, considered the destruction of Jerusalem to be a punishment by God for the sins of the people. The Jewish Christians, conversely, saw the destruction as the final departure of the scepter from Israel. The loss of the Temple meant that Judaism now had only the law as a basis for continued independence.

Had the Jewish Christians been the only members of the new faith, the breech between them and the orthodox Jews might have been healed, Both the Jewish followers of Jesus and the orthodox faction, desired to observe the law. But the Rabbis in Yavneh were aware that Hellenized gentile Christians, who did not feel it necessary to observe the law in its formal appearance, were in league with the Temple faction. There is historic evidence that the orthodox Jews knew about the teachings of Paul, and condemned them completely. Consequently, it was a short step from condemnation of Hellenized influences to formally refusing Jewish Christian acceptance in religious activities. That was the situation prior to Roman destruction of the great Temple. After the Romans destroyed Jerusalem and killed many of the surrounding inhabitants, relations between orthodox and Christianized Jews became a mute point. Only the memory of bad feelings remained.

The initial separation of orthodox Jews and Christianized Jews created hostilities that carried over to the gentile community, newly formed and struggling with Roman persecution. Even today there are many who do not understand Judaism as a legitimate expression of following the one God.

Non-Jews in communication with Christian Jews, already close to Judaism, very likely formed the first recognized group of converts to the new faith of Christianity These were the so called God fearers who accepted certain basic Jewish obligations. Called Noachide laws, this set of obligations was given for all people forbidding idolatry, the shedding of blood and grave sexual sins. Originally, the Synagogue accepted obligated gentiles who practiced the less rigorous Noachide precepts. It is likely the apostolic church of Jerusalem had accepted the view of the Synagogue on the place of the Noachide precepts. It was part of Jewish law that gentiles could follow the full extent of the Law, but it was also possible for gentiles to secure their salvation by following the less stringent Noachide precepts. They were not formally accepted as Jews, however, unless they fulfilled all the laws and commandments. The Christian God fearers, held this view as well, as we see from the Epistle to the Galatians. Many wished to observe as many Jewish precepts as they could. The leadership of the mother church in Jerusalem decided to lay no burden upon gentile believers beyond the Noachide precepts (Acts 10:28-29). It did not object to their voluntarily observing more, but required less. Among the figures of the primitive church who instructed gentile Christians to observe these precepts was Peter. Evidence of Paul's criticism of Peter regarding the gentiles confirms this. Rather than interpreting the Apostolic decree as a minimum, Paul evidently saw the Noachide precepts as the maximum obligation gentile Christians could practice. Paul, in his incident with Peter at Antioch says that *"No man is ever justified by doing what the Law demands, but only through faith in Christ Jesus, so we too have put our faith in Jesus Christ, in order that we might be justified through this faith and not through deeds dictated by Law; for by such deeds scripture says no mortal man shall be justified if righteousness comes by Law, then Christ died for nothing."* If this is what Paul thought about the Jewish way of life and worship, we can easily understand why he did not accept the view that gentile Christians should accept Jewish obligations.

While Paul was not the only Christian who opposed gentile Judaizers, he was the most influential. It should be historically noted that the liberation of gentile Christianity from the yolk of Jewish commandments was a necessary step for Christianity to become a cohesive religion, separate from Judaism. It is impossible to know whether Paul and other Christians of his time were even aware that by his teachings and letters he had helped to achieve this aim. He does not speak explicitly about the necessity of separating Christianity from its Jewish roots. It was only later in the second century we find Ignatius, writing to the Magnesians, stating that by the end of the first century those who had entered the Church ceased to observe the Sabbath on Saturday and celebrated it on Sunday. Some decades later, Justin Martyr expressed the personal view that Jewish Christians who observe the law could be considered brethren, provided they did not induce gentile Christians to be circumcised like themselves, or to keep the Sabbath or observe any related ceremonies. He also writes that there are gentile Christians who do not agree with him, extending hospitality to Jewish Christians who still observe the Mosaic law. At a later point, everything possible was done to prohibit the observance of the Law. The prohibition not allowing Law related observances was completed soon after these views were written. Ironcially, as the institutional Church developed, it too generated laws for its members to follow. While the Laws of Moses were set aside, new ones would identify the new faithful. It would appear Paul's belief alone position could not stand the scrutiny of history.

The end of the second century would witness the complete separation between the early Church and Synagogue. The unfortunate wall between the early Church and Synagogue would remain in place to this time.

Today, more than ever, we need to remove that wall, separating the two faiths. More than anything else, we need to remove the hostility and prejudice and resolve in every way to find a pathway to show that both faiths need each other and are a part of each other. Tension towards Judaism was a historical necessity for Christianity to become an independent world religion - a need, which no longer exists. Thus, what we do need today more than ever before, is to remove and break down the walls of ignorance and prejudice. By doing so, we will be able to bring harmony to both faiths.

Editor's Postscript

Rabbi Plotkin has given us a much needed glimpse into a period of history not widely tracked by the popular media. I would add my own perceptions, with his permission, that complement the excellent and long awaited work he has done.

If ever circumstances dictated what would become a historic nightmare for many millions of people destined to survive and triumph over insurmountable obstacles, it was the two decisions made by two different emperors of Rome. Not many people even know the name of Vespasian, emperor of Rome from 69 to 79, but his decision to put down the Jewish rebellion with the typical harshness of an angry dictator singularly set the stage for centuries of misery and misunderstanding. Vespasian ordered the full complement of troops to put down and destroy Jerusalem and its surroundings. The great second destruction of Jerusalem and the Temple within its gates, created the last Diaspora of the Jews, pushing them out of their homeland, religious center and beloved identity to become sojourners in many strange lands and at the mercy of other nationalities.

The second major decision of a Roman emperor came within a short time, in 135 of the Common Era. Hadrian, Roman emperor from 117 to 138 CE, responded to the second great Jewish insurrection by again ordering the full complement of troops to Judea to once more kill and put down any and all inhabitants of this land. He went even further than Vespasian had gone. He decreed, under penalty of death, all surviving Jews to forever be forbidden from returning to their beloved homeland. That ended the Jewish nation, any prospects of returning to the tradition of the Temple, and prevented an old morally respected religion from taking its rightful place among the other great religions.

Judaism is based on two historic events. First the life of father Abraham who is the father of a nation, an identifiable group of people forming around a promise. Second, the life of Moses who encounters the one God, bringing from his encounter the rules by which this people can live. Father Abraham is the father of a nation. Moses is the father of the religion. Both are honored as God appointed and God led. Both lead to a people who hold a rightful place in the larger world community with much to offer and much to add to how everyone can live and experience the greater beyond in their lives. The Jews, a name given to the people around Jerusalem in Judah, have held to both the promise and the gift of God through God's Law.

I believe the two events previously described, have been the chief contributors to anti-Semitism and societal persecutions. They are not the only ones as you may have discovered by reading this far. The Byzantine Church, even before emperor Constantine decreed Christianity to be the legitimate religion of the now Christian Empire, showed clear signs of rejecting anything Jewish. How much of this was motivated by a misreading of the newly formed Christian scriptures is hard to say. How much was a direct result of prior orthodox rejections of gentile converts is questionable, even while in the mix. But what followed, would never have done so were it not for those two decisions made toward the end of the first century and soon into the next century.

Without a homeland, compelled to survive in someone's else's country, the Jews turned inward and courageously held to what was most precious to them, their religious identity. It is a story more miraculous than any novel could tell. Overcoming the greatest of obstacles created by a misunderstanding of the Christian texts and human greed, the Jews have triumphed to this new century, maintaining a compass for all humanity to emulate. They have indeed become a light to the gentiles.

Historically, it is not difficult to trace the negative effects of sojourning in a strange land. Having a strange language, which contributed to maintaining their religious and cultural identity, the Jews discovered that other peoples, not schooled in this difficult language of Hebrew often saw it as one more reason not to trust these people. Not having the same rights as others born in those nations, the Jews quickly discovered that what they could achieve, could easily be taken from them at great human cost. Not trusting people who didn't agree with you and not having a national identity to draw from, forced these incredible people to support one another to the exclusion of strangers, a practice not encouraged by the religion of Judaism where strangers are treated with compassion and openness. The unfair treatment by gentiles, neither understanding nor approving the greatness of a gifted people, has had its effects over the centuries. Jealousy, uncalled for hatreds and unfair competition have hardened a victimized people to whom the other two great Western religions owe most of their teachings.

What the world would look like today, had Vespasian and Hadrian not called the troops to Jerusalem, joins with so many other "what if" stories. But if you want to conjecture about it, you might begin with the assurance that most persecutions would never have happened, most incidences of religious and political actions motivated by fear and greed, would never have taken place. Perhaps, Islam's incredible advancements in the 6th and 7th centuries would have moved around Israel, instead of through it. Judaism may even have changed its shape to include Jesus' teachings and his self discovered role of bringing people back to God. Instead of two related faiths there might even be one today. It is something to consider.   K.P. -Editor

Suggested Readings

Bartlett, John R. *I Maccabees*
(Sheffield Academic Press, Sheffield, 1998)

Beker, J. Christian. *Paul the Apostle*
(Fortress, Philadelphia. 1984)

Betz, Hans Dieter. *"First and Second Corinthians,"* in Anchor Bible
Dictionary, Vol. 1 (Doubleday: new York, 1992) ps. 1139-1154

Briggs, R.C. *Interpreting the New testament Today*
(Abingdon Press, Nashville, 1973)

Bristow, John Temple. *What Paul Really Said About Women*
(Harper & Row, San Francisco, 1988)

Bultman, Rudolph, *Primitive Christianity in Its Contemporary Setting*
(Meridian, New York, 1956)

_____.*Jesus Christ and Mythology*
(Macmillian, New York, 1981)

Callon, Terrance, *Forgetting the Root: The Emergence of Christianity
from Judaism* (Paulist Press, New York, 1986)

Charlesworth, James H. *"Old Testament Apocrypha,"* in Anchor Bible
Dictionary, Vol. I (Doubleday, New York, 1992) ps.292-294

Coggan, Donald. *Paul: Portrait of a Revolutionary*
(Crossroad, New York, 1985)

Collins, John J. *Jewish Wisdom in the Hellenistic Age*
(Westminster/John Knox, Louisville, 1997)

Desila, David A. *4 Maccabees*
(Sheffield Academic Press, Sheffield, 1998)

Duling, Dennis. *Jesus Through History*
(Macmillian, New York, 1979)

Fredriksen, Paula. *From Jesus to Christ: The Origins of the New
Testament*
Images of Jesus (Yale University Press, New Haven, 1988)

Fitzgerald, John T. *"Philippians,"* in Anchor Bible Dictionary, vol. 1
(Doubleday: New York, 1992) ps. 318-326

Furnish, Victor Paul. *"Colossians,"* in Anchor Bible Dictionary, Vol.1
(Doubleday, New York, 1992) ps. 1090-1096

Grabbe, Lester L. *An Introduction to First-Century Judaism*
(Clark, Edinburgh, 1996)

Keener, Craig. *Paul, Women and Wives*
(Hendrickson, Peabody, MA, 1992)

178

Malherbe, Abraham J. *Paul and the Thessalonians: The Philosophic Tradition of Pastoral Care* (Fortress Press, Philadelphia, 1987)

Meeks, Wayne A. *The First Urban Christians: The Social World of the Apostle Paul* (Yale University Press, New Haven, 1983)

Metzger, Bruce M. *An Introduction to the Apocrypha* (Oxford University Press, New York, 1957)

_____ *The Apocrypha of the Old Testament* (Oxford University Press, New York, 1977)

Morrow, Stanley B. *Paul: His Letters and Theology: An Introduction to Paul's Epistles* (Paulist Press, New York, 1986)

Myers, Charles D. *"Romans,"* in Anchor Bible Dictionary, vol. 5 (Doubleday, New York, 1992) ps. 816-830

Nolan, Albert. *Jesus Before Christianity,* (rev. ed.) (Orbis Press, Maryknoll, NY, 1992)

Pelikan, Jaroslav. *Jesus Through the Centuries: His Place in History and Culture* (Yale University Press, New Haven, 1985)

Quinn, Jerome D. *"Timothy and Titus, Epistles to..."* in Anchor Bible Dictionary, vol.6 (Doubleday, New York, 1992) ps. 560-571

Roetzel, Calvin. *The Letters of Paul: Conversations in Context* (John Knox, Atlanta, 1991)

Roetzel, Calvin J. *The World That Shaped the New Testament* (John Knox, Atlanta, 1985)

Russell, D. S. *Between the Testaments* (S.C.M. Press, London, 1960)

Sanders, E.P. *Paul* (Oxford University Press, Oxford, 1991)

Segal, Alan E. *Paul the Convert: The Apostolate and Apostasy of Saul the Pharisee* (Yale University Press, New Haven, 1990)

Segundo, Juan Luis. *The Historical Jesus of the Synoptics,* John Drury, translator(Orbis Books, Maryknoll, NY, 1985)

Senior, Donald. *Jesus: A Gospel Portrait,* new and rev. ed. (Paulist Press, New York, 1992)

Sparks, H.F.D. *The Apocryphal Old Testament* (Oxford University Press, Oxford, 1984)

Talbert, Charles H. *Reading Corinthians: A Literary and Theological Commentary on I and II Corinthians* (Crossroad, New York, 1987)

Winston, David. *The Anchor Bible Commentaries, The Wisdom of*

Printed in the United States
15775LVS00005B/42

9 780971 382336